A Handbook for

Deputy Heads

in Schools

A Handbook for
Deputy Heads
in Schools

Second **Edition**

Jim **Donnelly**

**KOGAN
PAGE**

To my mother

First published in 1991
Second edition published in 1999

Apart from any fair dealing for the purposes of research or private study, or criticism or review, as permitted under the Copyright, Designs and Patents Act 1988, this publication may only be reproduced, stored or transmitted, in any form or by any means, with the prior permission in writing of the publishers, or in the case of reprographic reproduction in accordance with the terms of licences issued by the Copyright Licensing Agency. Enquiries concerning reproduction outside those terms should be sent to the publishers at the undermentioned address:

Kogan Page Limited
120 Pentonville Road
London N1 9JN

© Jim Donnelly, 1991, 1999

British Library Cataloguing in Publication Data

A CIP record for this book is available from the British Library.

ISBN 0 7494 2877 5

Typeset by Saxon Graphics Ltd, Derby
Printed and bound by Biddles Ltd, Guildford and King's Lynn

CONTENTS

ACKNOWLEDGEMENTS

I would like to thank: Shirley, for her patience and help; colleagues and students, past and present, for their inspiration and my NPQH students, who showed how far management has come on in our schools in recent years.

INTRODUCTION

Since the first edition of this book was written, there has been nearly a decade of change in schools. The result is that the following quotation holds more truth today than it did then: 'effective management is the key to more effective schools and that deputy heads have a vital role to play as members of senior management teams'. Local Management of Schools has altered many things. A significant change for readers of this book is in the nature of deputy headship: senior management teams are now firmly established, not only in secondary schools, but also in primary schools, with the result that there are more people than ever acting in senior management roles. While there may be fewer deputy heads than ten years ago (particularly in secondary schools), there are now more staff involved in decision-making at senior level. This book is of relevance to all members of senior management teams, whatever their title.

The recurrent theme of the book is that there is a vast amount of human potential among the staff of a school and that its release depends on the quality of management. The importance of senior management is well documented and does not need to be restated, but the complexity of the work involved means that the nature of the team does need clear thinking and clear policies in our schools. In addition to being a guide for senior managers, therefore, this book is also intended to continue to serve in a sense as a rallying cry for teamwork in our schools.

The task of the senior management team is to motivate staff so that their potential is unlocked, and then to manage this explosion of energy in a productive, focused way. We live in an age where the status quo is not acceptable, and therefore schools find themselves having to constantly look for improvement on a year by year basis. The choice is to go forward or to fall behind.

Most people will choose to go forward, provided that they have the confidence and competence to do so; whether or not they have these attributes depends on the senior managers. The responsibility is considerable, but so is the reward when we see young people achieving to their full potential.

The masculine pronoun is used throughout the book from the desire to avoid ugly or cumbersome language: this should not be taken to imply any lack of commitment to equality of opportunity for all staff, which is vital in schools.

SENIOR MANAGER

Is my team ploughing?
(A E Housman)

There are few schools nowadays that do not operate a Senior Management Team (often known as the 'SMT' for short). However, it would be wrong to assume that SMTs are a homogeneous species: observation of how they operate shows that there is tremendous variety in both the nature of the teams and the range of responsibilities devolved to their individual members.

Even where there is an extended SMT (including other senior members of staff), there is often a smaller one consisting of the head teacher and deputies. The fact that this team may have agreed in some places not to take major policy decisions without reference to the extended senior management grouping does not alter the fact that there is an ultimate responsibility vested in the head, which passes to deputies in the head's absence. This smaller team (and the extended one, where it exists) is where the deputy will find himself when he takes up his new, senior management, role. In a primary school – and in some secondary schools as well – there may be only one deputy; if this is the case, it is vital that the deputy is aware that he could be required to take over as acting head without notice – and for weeks if not months in some cases.

AN INCREASED LEVEL OF RESPONSIBILITY

The most noticeable thing about becoming a deputy head is that you take on a much greater level of responsibility, and this is why you are paid more – not because you are more dedicated or in some way intrinsically better than the rest of the staff. Your colleagues – both teaching and non-teaching staff – will think of you as 'senior management', 'the powers that be', or even 'them'! You will be asked for views or decisions on a much wider range of issues than you have been used to and what you say will carry greater import. What you think of as a casual opinion may be taken as a pronouncement of senior management policy. For example, during a period of trade union action one particular group of staff may be taking action with which you do not agree. In the past, no doubt, you would have offered your own opinion in the staff room about what they were doing, which may have caused some ill-feeling but no more. If, on the other hand, you voice such an opinion now that you are a deputy, it may well be taken as the view of 'senior management', which could lead to (at best) a trip by the union representatives to the head to clarify the position or (at worst) a walk-out.

The question of expectation is one with which you need to come to terms. You may have been fortunate enough, as many deputies are these days, to have been given some senior management responsibilities in your previous position, but even then you will not have carried the same level of responsibility at all times. For example, as a member of a senior management committee you will have tried to represent all departments, but for most of the time you will have been exercising your middle-management role as a head of mathematics, languages or whatever (in a secondary school) or as something such as co-ordinator for Key Stage 2 (in a primary school), either of which will have given you some responsibilities over some staff for some of the time. The difference when you become a deputy is that you exercise senior management responsibilities all of the time. You cannot pass the buck to 'senior management' – you are part of 'them' now!

Role or task?

This is an appropriate point at which to look at the distinction between 'role' and 'task'. 'Role', I suggest, refers to what deputies do as a result of their position, while 'task' refers to specifically delegated activities, such as preparing the timetable, managing staff development or preparing the budget.

Having suggested this distinction, I would like to warn against taking it too far. Some zealots have become so obsessed with highlighting the importance of 'role' that they seem to have forgotten that part of the way in which a role is defined is by actually doing something, ie undertaking tasks. You may have a very grand idea of your sense of importance and talk proudly of your role, but if you do not actually *do* anything it is hard to see how you are helping to further the mission of the institution.

From captain to coach

The change of role up to deputy head may be thought of as moving on from being captain of a sports team to being its coach or 'player-coach'.

You have been captain – of a departmental, pastoral or curricular team – and you have quite clearly not moved to the position of full team manager, which includes making the final decisions about team selection. You do, however, bring a wealth of experience to your job and you form part of the central decision-making group within the school.

Different head teachers. like sports team managers, exercise their functions in different ways, and this determines to a large extent your level of real responsibility within the organisation. You may be consulted on 'team selection' – new appointments to the school – and you may have a real input into other important decisions on the curriculum, student discipline, and identification of school priorities. However, you are not the 'manager' and can ultimately be overruled by the head teacher. (If you find this happens to you a lot, it is time to sort it out by discussion with the head.)

A valuable team player

You also have to get used to the idea that you are a junior player again, for at least two teams: the senior management team and possibly a departmental team. It may have been some time since you have found yourself in that position. If you do not give the matter some thought, it could take you quite a long time to make the appropriate adjustments, if in fact you ever manage to do so.

You may have had a member of the senior management team working within your department, pastoral or curricular team in the past. You may have even resolved that when you became a deputy head you would not fail to attend departmental meetings, decline to take on responsibility for a year group, or whatever. Now is the time to put principle into practice, but you may not find it as easy as you imagined!

Another aspect of this is that you will have to get used to asking for certain things on the timetable (in a secondary school) or taking a particular year group (in a primary school) but not necessarily getting them. You may find, for example, that the head of department is keen to allocate 'A' level teaching to other members of the department; you may even find that your senior status means that you are seen as being 'good' with potentially awkward groups of students. Where top 'sets' operate, you may not get one – ever! In the primary school, the head may feel that your seniority is needed in a particular year group.

You are also a junior member of the senior team. While sorting out your position within the departmental team does require some thought, it is something over which you have some control and your attitude to your head of department can alleviate many potential problems. However, your position within the senior management team will be more complicated. Much of this complication centres round the definition of 'team'.

John Stuart Mill suggested that the 'Worth of a State ... is the worth of the individuals composing it'. This addresses the central issue of teamwork: how far can the individual find self-expression within a team? If a team consists of clones of the head – whatever type of person he or she may be – then it will be severely limited in its ability to contribute to the continuous growth of the school. If you think of the most consistently successful teams, whether in schools, in business or on the playing field, you will notice that they have an ability to harness individual talent for the common good. To do this, they need to achieve a balance between the needs of the individual and the needs of the team.

Your difficulty is that you are not the team captain. You may have had very successful experience as an academic or pastoral head, practising teamwork and exercising a strong leadership role. However, you are not the captain of the SMT and it will be very unusual indeed if your captain – the head – is exactly the same kind of leader that you were in your earlier role(s). As suggested above, most schools claim to operate senior management teams, but 'our team' in one school will probably differ greatly in practice from 'my team' in another.

Part of the reason for this must be laid at the door of perception. There are as many perceptions of how good a team is as there are members of the team plus members of the public! To some extent, every individual in every team has to devise his own *modus vivendi*, but I would like to offer one approach that may be helpful in seeking your own answers to the teamwork question.

RIGHTS AS WELL AS RESPONSIBILITIES

The approach I suggest here balances rights against responsibilities. So if you are expected to help implement a policy on, for example, school uniform or an assessment policy, then you can reasonably expect that you have a right to a proper say in the decision-making process. (If you go to a school where there is already such a policy, you cannot expect it to be reviewed specially for your arrival – but in this case, surely you checked before accepting the post.) If you are expected to attend PTA meetings, you have a right to be told this, preferably before accepting the post; you should not have to guess! If you are expected to take responsibility for staff development, you have a right to be involved in the initial selection procedure. The corollary of this is that if you are properly involved in the decision-making process – say, for example, on the question of school uniform or revising the assessment policy – then you have the responsibility to try to implement the agreed policy. These examples indicate the ways in which you can use the rights–responsibilities model to work out your position within a senior management team.

There are two rights that you share with all staff: the right to a job description and the right to some kind of appraisal. You have a legal right to both. At the time of writing (1998), your conditions of service differ from those of other staff (with the exception of the head) in that the 1265 hours of 'directed time' do not apply to you. However, the test of reasonableness does apply to anything that you may be asked to do.

If you feel that you are not being treated as an equal member of the team, you should first of all clarify in your own mind exactly what you expect and what you are not receiving. If you are clear that there are certain reasonable expectations that are not being met, then you should arrange to see the head and make him aware of this. As with most things, the best hope for positive advance is a situation where you can discuss the matter calmly, and this should be your aim. However, real life is not always like this!

The only thing that I can say here is that ultimately your own personal sense of worth is so inextricably linked with being a teacher that there may come a time when you need to consider making a major career decision if your situation is affecting your ability to do your job and lead a fulfilling life outside school. This does not mean either that you have failed or, indeed, that the rest of the team is at fault: sometimes teams just do not work effectively, and this can be said without apportioning blame.

ACTING FOR THE HEAD

There will be times when you are delegated to act on behalf of the head. This can happen for part of a day, for instance where a senior-staff duty system operates, or for longer when the head is out of school for some time. If the school is properly organized, many decisions are automatically taken by teaching and/or non-teaching staff during the day without reference to the head (or to you if you are acting as head). However, on occasion you may be called upon to make a decision, not as yourself but as acting head of your particular school.

In such cases, it should always be your aim to act in the way that is agreed by the team and the school: there may be ways in which you would change the school given the opportunity, but acting for the head for a day or two is not the time to do this. (Of course, if there is effective team management in operation, the head will not have to worry about letting you loose on his or her school!) Whether you choose to use the head's car parking space (if such peculiarities exist in your school) or to take over the head's office (complete with your tray of begonias) is a matter of personal judgement.

REPORTING TO THE TEAM

There are three main areas where, as a member of the SMT, you may need to report back to the team. The first of these is in the day-to-day running of the school; the second is where you have responsibility for a particular part of the school (eg lower or upper school, a school site, or a group of curriculum areas); and the third is where a specific task is delegated to you (eg timetabling, pastoral system, finance, buildings, literacy, numeracy). Your method of reporting back should take account of the different nature of the delegation.

Daily operation of the school

In larger schools, many management teams meet for daily briefings to discuss what has been happening and what is due to happen. This will range from activities such as parents' evenings and expected visitors to the school, to what has been happening with particular students and/or staff during the day. If the briefings are held each morning, the review will obviously be of the previous day's happenings.

Such reporting is essential if a team approach is to work, since otherwise several members of the team may deal with one particular part of a situation without knowing what each other is doing. This kind of meeting will focus on day-to-day events, and the implementation of policy rather than its formulation. If a major issue is identified during one of these meetings, then time needs to be set aside in a longer meeting for more considered debate and action. Such meetings need to be planned in advance, with a set agenda and associated briefing papers. There is more in Chapter 10 on meetings in general, which is as relevant to SMT meetings as any other – although it is surprising that in some schools all meetings are run efficiently except the senior management ones!

Responsibility for a part of the school

Where you have responsibility for a particular part of the school, whether it be the lower school, the nursery, the south site or the maths/science/

technology areas, other members of the team need regular feedback on what is going on there. Such feedback can be undertaken in relation to particular events that day (for example, notification that a local dignitary will be in school, or that local junior-school children are visiting) or at regular management meetings (for example, news that a new initiative is planned). Good lines of communication are essential between members of a team, not only on small details but also on broader issues – particularly since the latter will often impinge on the specific tasks of others.

Specific delegated tasks

It is important that a balance is struck between every member of the team knowing every detail of what everybody else is doing – which will not be a lot if they spend all day on such feedback – and everybody ploughing his or her own furrow. It is certainly wise to use your senior colleagues as sounding boards for ideas that you intend to put to staff, because this can often improve the detail of a proposal to staff and can save their time because it has been carefully considered first. A practical example would be where you were given the responsibility of organizing duty teams. It would create problems if you were to issue instructions that countermand the practice of the past twenty years regarding which side of the path students must walk on when entering and leaving school. However, such difficulties are easily avoided by showing a draft of your proposals to colleagues, who will hopefully alert you of any possible *faux pas*.

Another fairly easy and effective way of keeping team members up-to-date is to have a slot at each senior management meeting for each team member to report – briefly – what is going on. This briefing could cover such items as the timetable, building repairs, liaison with other schools, etc.

MANAGEMENT VERSUS ADMINISTRATION

Your teaching commitment as a deputy head will almost certainly be smaller than you have been used to – most deputies seem to range from a 25 per cent to a 40 per cent teaching load – in recognition of your new and additional management responsibilities. In Chapter 11 we look in more detail at how you can manage your time and deal with administration, but the point that should be made here is that you need to distinguish clearly in your own mind between management and administration. Believe it or not, Form 7 (an annual return to the DfEE that details pupil and staff members, destination of the previous year's leavers, and so on) is a source of solace for many deputy heads since the results are measurable and many staff view this as 'real' work: plenty of 'brownie points' all round!

If you stop to think – which is vital – it may occur to you that administration is not a job you should be doing at all. A clear distinction needs to be made between taking responsibility for something – the management function – and actually doing it in every little detail – the administration function. (This can be difficult in a small school, where there may only be a part-time secretary, and in such cases its governors may well need to consider whether the staff need more clerical support.) Remember that you are paid primarily to *manage* and this should be your priority.

A word to the wise

One danger inherent in your new position is that you will see so many possibilities that you may become overwhelmed by your desire to change the whole world all at once. You may even come to believe that it is possible. It is not!

POINTS TO NOTE

❏   You are now a senior manager.
❏   You belong to a team.
❏   People have certain expectations of you.
❏   You have rights and responsibilities.
❏   You are paid to manage.
❏   You are not God.
❏   Even the head is not God!

2

MANAGING STAFF

O brave new world, that has such people in it
(William Shakespeare)

Reference has already been made to the expectations that other people will have of you in your new role, and these need to be taken into account in thinking of how you will undertake your role as a senior manager in the school. More important to begin with, however, is to give some thought yourself to how you intend to act as a senior manager.

As a full-time teacher, you will have been leading by example in the classroom; as a middle manager, you will have had to work with other members of staff to achieve the aims of the departmental, pastoral or curricular team. As a senior manager, you will be less able to do things on your own; much of the time you will be seeking to achieve your aims through other people. You need to think this through and devise ways of working within this new situation.

To complicate matters further, you will also have more direct contact with non-teaching staff in a managerial sense; and you will quickly realize that non-teaching staff are not a homogeneous group of people! One thing they do have in common with all staff is that encouragement can work wonders in raising morale and performance.

In Chapter 8 we look in detail at staff development from the perspective of deputy heads who have this responsibility delegated to them. It may be helpful here to look at how all deputies can manage with different categories of staff, with the caveat that the mission of the school will only be achieved by all the people within it if they are working with a common sense of purpose. To a large extent this will happen only when we stop thinking of the staff of a school as discrete elements who inhabit the same building but instead as members of one large team.

TEACHER-COLLEAGUES

You have general and specific functions with regard to your teacher-colleagues. They will all perceive you to be a senior manager within the school. You will be asked for advice on occasions – perhaps for dealing with a staff problem – and even for permission to do things, such as going out of school. It is well to be prepared for this in advance, since it is almost certainly something that has not been part of your previous middle-management role.

Acting as coach

It was suggested in Chapter 1 that you will be performing a role akin to that of a sports team coach. Your colleagues will recognize that you do not have the ultimate decision in many instances, but they will also see you as having a significant degree of influence in the final decision-making process; they will therefore seek to influence you. A wise head of department/house/year or Key Stage co-ordinator will involve senior staff in praising students' achievements and in dealing with particularly recalcitrant individuals. While you are doing this, they will be, either consciously or unconsciously, drawing your attention to areas of need and to actions that the senior management team could take to improve working conditions.

You also have a role the other way round – in influencing *them* and in spreading the views that the SMT espouses. A simple example is the priority given to teaching. If the head and deputies decide that they should only be disturbed in their classrooms in an extreme emergency – and a good senior management team can set this standard quite easily – this will reinforce the belief that teaching is seen as very important and will encourage staff to share this belief.

It is perhaps a counsel of perfection for deputies to get to their lessons on time – telephone calls to the local education authority or contractors are often returned just as the bell has gone (and the heating will only work if you take the call!) – but punctuality should be achieved whenever possible. An explanation of why you have been late may sound a bit lame but it should be given anyway, at least to the colleague who looked after your class for you, if not to the class itself. You may also be asked on occasion by the head to speak to a teacher who arrives late for his/her lessons and your own example in setting a high priority in getting to your lessons on time makes this easier to do.

Confidentiality

You will sometimes find yourself, as a deputy head, being told something in confidence that creates problems for you. The first thing to say is that the safest thing is to assume that anything you have been told is in confidence. If you hear the same information (for example, that a particular member of staff is having problems at home) repeated generally in the staff room, then it is reasonable to assume that it was not told to you in confidence – but it is still best that you should not be the source of it.

The kind of information that creates problems is where a member of staff tells you something in confidence that cannot really be taken as such: s/he may, for example, tell you that s/he has hit a student, which is obviously a disciplinary matter. Your best approach to this kind of revelation is to try to persuade the teacher concerned to report the matter formally, either to yourself or to the head. If such persuasion does not work, then you have little choice but to report the matter to the head yourself.

If this seems like a betrayal of confidence, it may be useful to consider that you have been asked to do something that is unreasonable: if you had been aware of the nature of the revelation, then it is likely that you would have refused to grant confidentiality to the conversation in the first place. You certainly cannot pretend that you did not hear the conversation, which may be suggested to you when it becomes clear that you are not prepared to keep the matter to yourself.

One other point worth making about this type of approach by a member of staff is that you should always advise him/her to speak to the school representative of his/her professional association. Disciplinary matters have usually clear and agreed procedures, which are intended to benefit all parties, including the school.

Having a private word

If it is *you* who wants to have a 'private word' with someone, it should be exactly that: private. It is not always easy to avoid being drawn into a public debate on what should be a private matter, partly because this can be a useful tactic for a particular member of staff in trying to make some point, but it should be avoided if possible.

There are occasions when you have to undertake an unpleasant task such as speaking to a member of staff about attendance or punctuality – possibly at the request of the head, who does not want to institute more formal disciplinary proceedings if they can be avoided – and to do this in public is wrong. It is also crucial that you make clear exactly what you are talking about. It is false kindness to ask to speak to someone about their poor attendance record and not then to make clear that there is at the very least a potential problem. Such comments should be made without rancour, for as a manager you are seeking to improve performance not to lessen it. If you feel uncomfortable, say so, but do not then diminish the importance of what you are saying.

Acting as adviser

As you become established in the school your teacher-colleagues will form opinions on how useful or otherwise your advice is on a wide range of matters, from teaching techniques to domestic crises. You will ideally be seen as non-partisan – as a former head of department or coordinator, say, you need to establish that you are not partial to one department's or one area's needs, and you should be able to offer opinions based on a broad view of the school's needs and from a perspective of someone who is an experienced teacher.

Very often, your main function will be to defuse situations and to offer a calm, rational approach to a problem that has been taken out of proportion. You need to strike the balance between demonstrating such calmness and seemingly not taking the situation seriously enough. Always remember that any difficult problem is made much worse if the senior team joins in the general sense of panic: you need to stay calm, while at the same time taking care to show that specific issues are being addressed and definite steps are being taken. Sometimes, it should be added, the solution might be to change the staff's perceptions of the particular situation: for some people, students have never been as poorly disciplined or as idle as this year's lot!

Where your advice is sought on non-teaching matters, it is often best to listen and to try to help the member of staff to work out a solution for himself or herself. Sometimes, of course, you can take specific action within school to give a colleague breathing space (relieving him/her of some teaching for a while, for instance) and you should do this wherever possible. There may well be occasions, frustrating as it can be, where there is not much more you can do.

Acting as an employment referee

You may be asked to act as an employment referee for a member of staff. It is almost certain that the head will have also been asked, since most potential employers in education require such a reference. It is not unusual for you to be asked, in that most jobs require two or three referees. For a junior member of staff in a secondary school, it is more usual for the second reference to be requested from the head of department, but middle managers in particular sometimes ask a deputy to be their second referee.

Ms Freda White
Head Teacher
Another School
ANOTHER TOWN
AN10 2HU

Dear Ms Brown,

Re: request for a reference for John Gillespie

I am replying to your request for a reference for John Gillespie in connection with his application for the post of Deputy Head Teacher at Another School. I have known John for the five years during which he has been at This School, a 11–18 comprehensive school with 1230 pupils on roll. He came to us with a strong reputation, which he has enhanced by his work here.

John is first and foremost an excellent teacher, who leads his department by example, engendering a positive working atmosphere example in his classroom and gains the respect of the students. He is very committed and can build very strong relationships with individual students. This influence is felt throughout his department, and staff have confidence in feeling supported in their work.

The Science department has developed under John's leadership. The Science curriculum has been reviewed and adapted, particularly in response to the National Curriculum. An interest in, and enthusiasm for, Science has been generated throughout the age range, and the numbers taking Science courses in the sixth form has increased; this includes students across the ability range. There has been a welcome increase in the numbers of girls opting for 'A' level Physics, due to the department's vigorous attempts to encourage this. Examination results are very good.

As already indicated, the staff respond very positively to John's leadership. He encourages them and supports them when necessary. He is tactful at dealing with other departments in consultative meetings, such as the finance committee. His administration of finance and examination entries is meticulous but unfussy, with deadlines invariably being met. Latterly he has been part of the senior management committee and has shown an ability to take a school-wide view on educational matters. He has actively sought to develop his knowledge, most recently by taking a management diploma at Any University.

I rate John very highly and strongly recommend that you interview him.

Yours sincerely

Jane Elliott, BEd,
Deputy Head Teacher

Figure 2.1 *Example of reference (secondary level)*

Ms Freda White
Head Teacher
Another School
ANOTHER TOWN
AN10 2HU

Dear Ms Brown,

Re: request for a reference for John Gillespie

I am replying to your request for a reference for John Gillespie in connection with his application for the post of Deputy Head Teacher at Another School. I have known John for the five years during which he has been at This School, a 3–11 primary school with 371 pupils on roll. He came to us with a strong reputation, which he has enhanced by his work here.

John is first and foremost an excellent teacher, who engenders a positive working atmosphere in his classroom and gains the respect of his pupils. He is very committed and can build very strong relationships with individual students. This influence is felt throughout the junior department, where he holds the responsibility for the co-ordination of our literacy and numeracy strategies, and staff have confidence in feeling supported in their work.

Both literacy and numeracy have improved substantially since John took on these responsibilities. The SATs results are very good and the numbers achieving Level 3 or below has dropped significantly.

As already indicated, the staff respond very positively to John's leadership. He encourages them and supports them when necessary. He is tactful at dealing with other staff members in consultative meetings, such as the finance committee. His administration of SATs arrangements is meticulous but unfussy, with deadlines invariably being met. Since he came to the school, he has been part of the senior management committee and has shown an ability to take a school-wide view on educational matters. He has actively sought to develop his knowledge, most recently by taking a management diploma at Any University.

I rate John very highly and strongly recommend that you interview him.

Yours sincerely

Jane Elliott, BEd,
Deputy Head Teacher

Figure 2.2 *Example of reference (primary level)*

The head should not find anything amiss about this – provided that s/he has also been asked! But you do have the problem of saying what is probably the same thing in a slightly different way. Figures 2.1 and 2.2 give examples of references you might write. In addition, I recommend that you always ask the member of staff for a brief note of the points that s/he has highlighted in her/his application, so that you do not miss out an important involvement in a project or particular aspect of work.

As a general rule, a reference should highlight achievements as specifically as possible. Furthermore, if you are asked about attendance and punctuality, you should give a quantifiable response as far as you can, and a particular absence that was untypical – say a spell off school with a broken leg – should be indicated. Above all, your reference should be honest and objective: it should concentrate on the subject's professional abilities and performance, not whether you find him/her congenial or not.

You should show the resulting reference to the teacher concerned. This has the double benefit of showing that you have actually done the reference and of showing her/him that s/he is valued in the event of not getting the promotion. If, however, the situation is such that you feel that your honest reference would be less than fulsome, say so as tactfully as possible and suggest the colleague ask someone else. Whereas the head has little choice but to provide a reference, you do have such a choice.

WORKING GROUPS AND COMMITTEES

It is likely that you will have to take responsibility for committees (eg INSET, finance, pastoral, literacy) and/or working groups (eg school day, individualized learning, assessment). There will be significant differences between doing this and chairing meetings in your previous middle-management role.

The first type of group will be the committee. This will usually be composed of representatives from different departments or Key Stages. Whereas your previous meetings may have consisted of people for whom you had direct line-management responsibility, the committee(s) you chair as a deputy head will be different. In the ideal situation, members of the committee will have been nominated by a department or another group of staff; they will be working to a specific brief, possibly allocating finance or implementing staff development policies; and they will be putting forward the points of view of those whom they represent. It is important that all staff know who serves on your committees and the rationale behind their composition.

Your role is to make sure that the committee meetings are effectively run (see Chapter 10), that decisions are taken, and that these decisions are both reported to all staff and carried out in practice. To ensure that there is a single, clear message given to all staff – instead of seven or eight slightly (or greatly) different ones – a report of decisions should be circulated to members of the committee and also to staff in general.

Some committees will have an indefinite life – INSET, finance, assessment, and so on – and you will find that they develop their own nature, partly depending on who happens to serve on them. After some time, you will find that attendance at them reinforces this feeling of belonging to a distinctive group. It is thus important that you seek the opinions of members of the group about how they feel it operates, and you should be prepared to change, for example, the times or format of meetings if necessary.

Working groups are different in that they are usually set up for a specific task, with a time limit on their deliberations. In this case it is particularly important that the task is seen to be done; otherwise members of the group will become frustrated and will find excuses to absent themselves. If you find yourself asked to chair a working group, get a clear mandate for what you are supposed to be doing: this will help your own sanity as well as that of your colleagues!

All the groups referred to above will have a whole-school focus. Individuals will represent particular interests, and it is your job to ensure that the needs of the school as a whole – which are ultimately the needs of the students – are constantly addressed. You should resist any suggestion that you represent a particular subject or the pastoral staff: you gave up doing that when you became a senior manager.

Serving as a committee member

As a deputy head you will also find yourself serving on committees or working parties *ex officio*. There may, for example, be an advisory committee covering both the academic and pastoral sides of the school, which meets periodically to advise on school policy. Where such a group exists for consultative purposes, you need to strike a balance between saying nothing and not allowing others to have an input to the process by continually replying to particular points as they arise. By the nature of your position, you will probably have more opportunities than they have to put your views forward; alternatively, if you sit silently all the time, others may think you are not interested, that the consultation is a sham, or that you actually have no ideas on anything. Such are the dilemmas that go with your position!

ON BEING HUMAN

We are all preoccupied from time to time in our daily working lives and may thus not acknowledge as readily as we ought to when we pass a colleague in a corridor. However, it is important to bear in mind that, as a senior member of staff, failing to at least nod to a colleague may be taken to be a sign of disapproval, particularly if you have disagreed at a meeting the last time you met. While not suggesting that you become Yeats' 'public, smiling man', you do need to be aware of this and to make a conscious effort to notice staff and to bid them the time of day. If you *are* in the habit of noticing staff, it is more likely that the few times you are so preoccupied that you rush past will be seen as untypical of you and will not be taken as a personal slight.

Another s castle

In spite of team teaching, it is most usual to find that the classroom, laboratory or gymnasium is seen as under the main control of a particular teacher at any given moment. If you enter someone else's classroom, make absolutely sure that you acknowledge this by your behaviour. Apart from upsetting a member of staff by storming into a classroom and behaving in a boorish manner, you will be unwittingly educating the students, who will all be watching and inwardly digesting how things are done.

In three decades of teaching, I have seen very few emergencies that have required a suspension of these basic civilities. This point goes back to that already made: staff and students learn from example – your example!

THE OFFICE

A significant change when you become a deputy head is your relationship with the 'office' staff. As a head of department or curriculum coordinator, you will have had dealings with the clerical staff, possibly having work typed or going through your delegated accounts, but there will have been days or even weeks when you may not have had to go into the school office at all.

When you become a deputy head this will almost certainly change. You will often be the first point of call when someone either telephones or comes into school asking to see a senior member of staff. You will have letters to be typed and you may have at least some clerical help with (among other things) finance, computer-based registers or assessment profiles. In some large schools you may find that the deputies have been allocated a specific secretary, while in others you will at least be able to call on their general services in a more particular way than you have been used to.

The office staff will expect you to take decisions in the manner in which a senior manager in business would: some of them will have worked in the world of business, giving them a wider perspective of management than many of us in education. If you have letters to be typed, you may be in a position of being able to specify that they are to take priority over some typing work left by other staff. You will also gain some insight into what is often a frenetic pace of work in the school office.

You have an important role to play in the interface between the teaching staff and clerical staff. Knowing the difficulties faced in their work by both groups of staff, you need to try to ensure that they see each other as mutually supportive in a common mission. Sometimes this interface can be fraught, which is a management problem: who will sort it out if not senior management?

You may be asked by the head to take particular responsibility for the office staff. Their work has been changed by the advent of the local management of schools (LMS) and management information systems. You need to be aware of how such systems affect their day-to-day working lives and of what training they need in order to adapt to what appear to be never-ending changes. (For instance, when a school that I worked in became involved in a pilot project for the use of a computer-based management information system, we were not prepared for the noise that the daisywheel printer would make and the result was that staff could not hear conversations clearly enough to work or to answer the telephone.) You should be aware that the office staff also have developmental needs and you should be prepared to argue their case with other members of the senior management team where necessary.

When you are involved in decision making with the teaching staff (for example, in developing records of achievement), you should remember not to presume to change the conditions of service of non-teaching staff without consultation. There are times when a particular change may not make much difference to teachers but might make a lot of difference to the way in which records are kept and the office works.

A different perspective

Indeed, it is often very informative and helpful to talk to the clerical staff about ways in which the school is run. They have a unique perspective and have very valuable comments to make if asked to do so. They also know a lot about the school that you do not. Sometimes they will have children at the school; at other times they will know something about particular children from their contact with them in the local community.

ANCILLARY STAFF

The term 'ancillary staff' is used to cover the work of a very wide range of employees, from caretakers to cleaners, from laboratory technicians to midday supervisors and learning support assistants. Under LMS and competitive tendering, some employees are now directly under the control of the school, while others are employed by a direct labour organization (DLO) or private contractor.

The general point that has already been made is that ancillaries will view a deputy head as a member of the senior management team, and this creates certain expectations of how you will act. It is very difficult to get to know every ancillary employee in a school right away, but you can usually at least guess when someone works there! The basic rule of acknowledging a fellow employee's existence and worth applies.

If you have specific complaints, or have complaints made to you by staff, about ancillaries, make sure that you know the line of management responsibilities before taking action. This is something you need to check carefully when you take up your deputy headship. You will not be very popular if you stir up one part of the staff because of your ineptitude or your failure to observe protocol. Having said this, you should not assume that there will be problems. Most schools are served by hardworking ancillary staff who are as keen as you are for the school to have a good name in the local community. After all, they probably live locally!

Chapter 9 deals in more detail with the responsibilities of the deputy head in charge of a site and/or its buildings. In these circumstances, a deputy will probably have a specific brief to liaise with the caretaking/cleaning staff.

POINTS TO NOTE

❑ All staff have a common mission.
❑ Everyone's job is important to the school.
❑ You need to manage with staff.
❑ You should have a whole-school perspective.
❑ Committees need to be purposeful.
❑ Acknowledge the existence and worth of colleagues.
❑ Encouragement can work wonders.

3

STUDENT CARE

Discipline   is   not for the benefit of the students
(Adam Smith)

Whether your students are 4, 11 or 18 you have a general duty of care towards them. As a deputy head there are three different ways in which this could involve you: as a teacher; in a general way supporting colleagues as a senior member of staff; and (depending on your job description) as the person responsible for what is generally known as 'the pastoral system'.

If the words of Adam Smith quoted at the beginning of this chapter are not to be true – and he suggested that discipline 'is contrived ... for the interest, or more properly speaking, for the ease of the masters' – then it is important that the school has clear, agreed policies on how student care is to operate. To some extent this is not entirely within your control, but your aim should be to ensure that the issue is addressed and resolved.

CARE AS A TEACHER

This book is not the place for a detailed consideration of the role of the individual teacher in the pastoral care system. However, it may be useful to draw attention to the point that your students ought neither to benefit nor to suffer because their teacher happens to be a senior member of staff.

Many deputies (and, indeed, heads) have found it helpful to try to operate in the classroom in the same way as any other member of staff would. They try to separate their senior management role from their teaching. So, for example, if a student is not working as well as he should, this will be referred to the head of department, who will then follow normal departmental procedures for such situations. There are several advantages in adopting this approach, apart from the fact that it is fairer to all students. The status of the head of department is enhanced in the eyes of both the staff and the students; and the deputy shows that teaching is not something that is suddenly perfected on becoming a member of the senior management team.

A point that needs to be made is that pastoral care is a means to an end: it exists not for its own sake but to enable students to achieve their full academic potential. The main purpose of being in a classroom is to help students to learn, not to impose 'discipline' upon them. Such learning requires a disciplined and orderly atmosphere, certainly, but the days have long gone when a teacher's primary function is to impose order on a large, potentially noisy rabble!

In my experience, the most successful learning takes place where the teacher approaches the task in the way described, as opposed to some kind of battle of wills. This is not, of course, to say that teachers do not have to concern themselves with discipline; I am merely trying to point out that the emphasis must be right.

CARE AS A SENIOR MEMBER OF STAFF

All teaching staff have a pastoral function outside their classroom. Where a system exists that formalizes and organizes this, the presence of any member of staff will have a noticeable effect on student behaviour. However, there are still schools where the first reaction to any 'discipline' problem is to refer it – either to a specific deputy or to any deputy who is available. This presumably is a throwback to the days when classes were large and a deputy was seen as the figure of authority/fear: one would hope that pedagogy has advanced since then! Having said this, there are occasions when the presence of a senior member of staff is important. Such a presence can be divided into supporting a teacher within a classroom and setting the tone outside.

Classroom support

Many staff appreciate the presence of a senior member of staff in their classroom, where such a presence is seen as routine and not threatening. It is important that the courtesies are observed and that the teacher's status and authority are not undermined: at that time you are a visitor to someone else's class and your demeanour should reflect this. (Later in the chapter we shall look at ways in which such support and visits can be built into the normal life of the school.)

There are times, however, when a different kind of support is needed. A particular member of staff may be struggling with the teaching function, for a variety of reasons. That teacher may ask for help, or it may be up to the senior management team to suggest it. It is often easier for a deputy head to undertake such support, since the head of department will usually have his or her own class to teach.

If such support is to be given, it should be discussed with the teacher; an agreement should be reached that makes clear what the support will be, how long it will last for, what specific objectives it has and what will happen after that. It is doing nobody – least of all the students – any favours to allow such a situation to drift along indefinitely, hoping (for example) for an early retirement to put an end to it.

There are also 'one-off' occasions where a member of staff needs an outsider to come in to the class and support him in establishing a calmer atmosphere. By responding to a request like this, it is clear that the teacher is still in control. You can use the opportunity to reiterate the view that students are in school to learn and that their behaviour is making this impossible, and so on.

Support around the school

The main task of any deputy is to set an example, both to staff and students. The way you speak to students will confirm or deny in their minds whether exhortations about civilized behaviour, people being of equal worth, and so on, are platitudes or guiding principles. There are times when it is perfectly proper to show annoyance – for example, if one student is attacking another – but the first aim in any difficult situation should be to calm both it and the participants. Once this has been done, an investigation can begin into what started the problem and what needs to be done about it.

Do not feel that it is necessarily your prerogative to do the investigation. Heads of house/year have perfectly proper rights in this regard. They may – or certainly should – know more about the individual students involved and should be able to take appropriate action.

Where the situation involves staff and students, it may be necessary for the deputy to deal with the investigation, but you will then need to seek the advice of tutor and/or head of house or year in dealing with it.

It should also be mentioned that while staff need to be supported, one should always remember the principles of justice, which the school no doubt espouses in its aims. Everything is not always sweetness and light in the real world and we all make mistakes; it follows that sometimes the main reason for a particular situation may owe as much to the member of staff's behaviour as the student's. This is where the existence of a clear and agreed philosophy is essential, for this allows staff to acknowledge human failings without feeling that they are total failures. They are not then so concerned about 'losing face', and may well be able to admit that the main responsibility was theirs; indeed, they usually gain respect from students for such an admission where it is genuine.

CARE AS A PASTORAL DEPUTY

Your job description may include overall responsibility for students' pastoral care. Try to ascertain before you accept the appointment whether this means overall responsibility for its organization and implementation or whether you are supposed to be some kind of 'hit man'. If it is to be the latter, consider carefully if this is really what you want to do with your professional training before accepting the post: it will be too late afterwards.

Assuming that the role can be viewed positively and that you are to be delegated the power to organize a proper pastoral care system, then you need to be clear in your own mind about your aims and objectives. Some suggestions are given here to help you establish your approach to this key element of any school.

Reward

Your first aim should be to establish that pastoral care will be based on a system of rewards. The age of the student needs to be taken into consideration – there are not many 17 year-olds who will still admit to wanting gold stars on their essays! – but all research indicates that achievement is greater where it is recognized. Such recognition may take the form of 'merit points' for 5- or 11-year-olds, or entries in a record of achievement for older students; but whatever form it takes, it should be built into the expectations of all students that achievement will be recognized as a matter of course.

There is, of course, overlap with the systems of rewards established by departments. Ideally, all rewards are gathered into a central record, with the key person here being the tutor. Since departmental rewards will almost certainly relate to academic achievement, you should aim to have non-academic achievement recorded also, particularly in the areas of co-operation and helping others; punctuality to school and regular attendance are particularly important, and the responsibility for recognizing and encouraging these aspects lies primarily with the tutor. Special activities such as taking part in a school play or a fund-raising walk should also be recorded.

Recognition

If students are not used to having their achievements formally recognized, it will take time to establish such a system. Some may find it embarrassing, particularly if there is peer-group pressure not be to seen as 'teacher's pet'. The key to success in this area is to ensure that the majority of students gain recognition (so that it is the minority who do not), instead of the other way round. The success of GCSE is the proof that the recognition of positive achievement does not lower standards, but actually raises them.

It is important to be aware that formal presentations at assembly can act as a disincentive to students to gain recognition: many of them do not want to be put on parade before the whole school. Some departments use senior staff to present academic achievement rewards in the less formal situation of the classroom – this is the kind of special attendance by a deputy referred to earlier, which can have the added advantage of creating an expectation that the presence of a deputy head in someone's classroom does not necessarily mean trouble! Some house or year groups have a separate assembly to present attendance/punctuality certificates, attended only by those receiving them.

One final point on this topic is that sending a letter home when a student has done something positive can act as a counterbalance to the times when one has to write home for other reasons. You should try to get a balance between such letters coming from tutors, from heads of house/year and from deputies; in all cases, tutors should know that they have been sent.

Setting up a reward and recognition system

Set out below are some ideas that may get you started in devising your own school's system of reward and recognition. They each aim to reward good effort by students and provide positive reinforcement of the achieving students' actions. The following are a few suggestions:

1. Verbal encouragement by teacher – the first and most important reinforcement.
2. Merit system – for effort, with awards (eg Gold, Silver, Bronze) when a certain number of points have been collected. Should be administered through tutors who can add their praise.
3. Award ceremony, possibly with a drink and a biscuit, limited to those receiving awards.
4. Referral to tutor, head of department and/or head of house/year for praise.
5. Letter home, particularly for younger students.
6. Referral to head or deputy head for praise.

7.   Award for good attendance, with realistic target (eg 95 per cent); for punctuality one might say no more than two times late per term (assuming a reasonable attendance rate).
8.   Subject awards, such as graded assessments. These can be presented in class by a deputy head or the head to give added status.
9.   Formal reports sent to parents – still very valuable!

Sanctions

Even when you have the reward and recognition culture firmly inculcated in the life of the school – and, you hope, spend a good deal of your time on the pleasant task of complimenting students for their achievements – there will still be situations that require the use of sanctions. As with rewards, there need to be guidelines on how lack of work, insolence, aggression and disruption should be dealt with. These guidelines need to include at least the following:

❏   examples of misdemeanours and suggested sanctions;
❏   details of actions that can and should be taken by individual members of staff;
❏   clear ideas of what needs to be referred further, and to whom.

The use of sanctions should be recorded, in a clear manner, for two reasons: first, the evidence may be needed in dealing with further offences; and, secondly, the tutor and head of house or year will be able to speak to the individual student and counsel or punish as appropriate.

It is easiest if a standardized form exists that all staff use to record the use of sanctions and that sets out clearly how it is to be routed: it should end up fairly quickly in the student's personal record file. A good idea is to use different colours of paper for complimentary and derogatory comments. Figure 3.1 gives an idea of the type of form that can be used: A4-sized paper is recommended, or alternatively double-sided A5 where the incident/concern is put on one side and the action taken/to be taken is put on the reverse. Do be aware of the need for the school to tailor its standard form to suit its own needs and culture.

The particular sanctions to be used are a matter for discussion within the individual institution. As far as possible, they should relate to the offence committed, should be understood by staff /students alike, and should be applied quickly. Above all, they should be consistent and just. A further comment will be made later about serious situations that involve parents visiting the school, but it is certainly wise to keep parents informed of offences that, if repeated, are likely to lead to more severe action.

INCIDENT/CONCERN FORM

Name of student: _____ *Tutorgroup:* _____ *Year:* _____

Name of teacher reporting incident/concern: _____

Nature of incident/concern:

Action taken so far:

Signature: _____ *Date:* _____

Referred to: _____

Comments/action taken:

Figure 3.1 *Example of incident/concern form*

CARE THROUGH OUTSIDE AGENCIES

As deputy in charge of the pastoral system you are likely also to be responsible for dealings with outside agencies, such as education welfare officers and educational psychologists. Your role here is to ensure that their skills and expertise are available to benefit the students of the school. Their perspectives will differ from the school's, but this should be seen as a benefit: sometimes we need our assumptions to be challenged, if only to allow us the opportunity to consider whether or not we are still doing what we think we ought to be doing.

You are the link between the classroom teacher and the various personnel from these student support services. It is important that at times you present what are opposing views on courses of action to both sides in the consultation process, and in a way that will lead to some measurable improvement in the performance of individual students. There are also *potential* conflicts that should not be ignored but resolved positively, and this is an area where your ability as a senior manager will be put to the test.

It is nevertheless particularly important that you do not see a quick, immediate solution to some of the school's problems by referring them to other agencies. The school needs to be clear about its own expectations and about the ways in which these can be achieved.

NATURAL JUSTICE

Whether or not you are the deputy head in charge of the pastoral system, you may well have to deal with situations that involve asking parents to come to school to discuss an issue, and/or excluding students from school. It is as well to be aware of the legal concept of 'natural justice', which becomes increasingly relevant with more formal disciplinary proceedings involving students.

The simple way of looking at the concept of 'natural justice' is to work on the basis that any action taken against a student by the school needs to be defensible in a quasi-legal setting. Such actions must therefore relate to offences committed and must not be capable of being construed as driven by malice. If a situation reaches a point where a student is being deprived of his education or being required to find another school, it is clear that this will have serious consequences for his educational future, and quite possibly for his whole life; once you start from this point, you will see very clearly the need for recording offences/actions from the start. For the vast majority of students, that situation will not be reached, but you do not know in advance which students it will apply to.

For a school, the concept of natural justice has several implications. These are primarily parental foreknowledge of a problem, the need for firm evidence of misdemeanour, and clear expectations of the school standard for a student's behaviour. Each of these is dealt with in more detail below.

Parental foreknowledge

There are few cases where drastic action needs to be taken that could not have been foreseen. If parents have not been notified of earlier problems, they have every reason to feel that the school has failed in its duty of care. Failure to inform them has also deprived the school of a potentially powerful force in modifying a student's behaviour. It can be tiresome writing to parents if you perceive that it is having no effect or if they refuse to come to school to discuss a problem, but it should be done even so and recorded punctiliously.

Evidence of misdemeanour

If a student may ultimately be asked to leave the school, it is essential that there is clear evidence available for any exclusion meeting and any possible appeal. It is much better if such evidence has been accumulated over a period of time, with a record of attempts made to improve the situation, including copies of letters to parents, records of home visits by staff and (hopefully) visits by parents to the school. It is also important that such problems are not seen as being located in a student's relationship with one particular member of staff.

In the case of any appeal hearing, written evidence will be crucial in showing the extent of the effort the school has made to prevent what cannot avoid being a severe disruption to a young person's education.

Clear expectations of behavioural standards

Staff and students alike should be aware of expected standards of behaviour, and also of likely sanctions in the event of such standards not being maintained. This surely requires some examples to be given of what are considered misdemeanours and what kinds of sanctions may be invoked. Such a set of standards would quite reasonably indicate that repeated offences would be treated more severely. The more it can be seen that there is a (downward) escalation the better, because this allows opportunities for the student to consider his or her behaviour and to improve before sanctions are imposed.

DEALING WITH EXTREME SITUATIONS

As a deputy head you are more likely to have to deal with what can sometimes be seen as an extreme and intractable situation. The best training you can have for this is to sit in when the head is dealing with such a case, before you have to deal with one yourself.

However, even in the absence of such training, you can do a lot to prepare yourself for such situations. There are likely to be four different scenarios, becoming progressively more complicated to deal with because an additional perspective and set of expectations is added each time. We look at these in turn below.

Disputes between students

The most straightforward of these difficult situations is likely to involve two or more students in serious disagreement with each other. Assuming that the heads of year/house have already unsuccessfully tried to resolve the situation, then it ends up with you for consideration. Perhaps the students concerned happen to be in the same class, they are implacable, they cannot be kept apart from each other even if this was felt to be a reasonable solution, the disagreement started somewhere back in the mists of time (I have been told by more than one 15 year-old that 'so-and-so' attacked me in infant school and has never liked me!), and has now reached the point where not only the protagonists but also the other people in their class cannot get on with their work. (Experience teaches that 18-year-olds are no better than 11-year-olds in this.)

The first rule is to allow each person involved to give an account of how he or she feels, without interruption. Once this has been done, you can try to summarize what you see as the situation. At this point, it is usually wise to forget your natural instinct of trying to make everybody like everybody else – it does not work with adults, and so it is not likely to work with children or young adults. What you do have to do is to establish the ground rules at the school that are designed to allow all students – including the ones in front of you – to get on with their work and to make academic progress.

You must be quite firm that, while accepting the rights of individuals not to like other individuals, their disagreements must no longer be allowed to interfere with the smooth running of the school and that any repetition of their disruptive behaviour will result in more severe action being taken. Your sympathies may lie with one or other of the protagonists – you are human as well – but that is not the issue you are dealing with in this particular example.

It can sometimes be useful to invite the parents to come in to the school in order to try to find a solution in conjunction with them. Be warned, however, that the problems may have started with them in the first place: the families may have lived near each other for a long time, they too might not like each other, and they may automatically side with their own child in the dispute. You nevertheless need to ensure that parents are made aware of the situation, and you need to state very clearly the school perspective referred to above.

Disputes between students and staff

The situation becomes more complicated when you have to resolve a conflict between one or more students and a member of staff. This problem may reach you as a complaint from the teacher/midday supervisor or from the student(s). In this case it is often wise to hear both sides of the story separately, so as to allow you to judge what actions are likely to be open to you.

Staff are entitled to expect that they will be supported, but students will also judge the school by how you deal with what they may feel to be a case of injustice. There is no obvious golden rule in dealing with this type of situation, particularly since the facts will usually differ from one case to the next. However, it would be unusual if you did not at some point get both parties together, if only to allow them to resolve the situation in the presence of a third party.

If you do this, your main function is to create a calm atmosphere, which will indeed help the situation to be resolved – you will often find that this atmosphere in itself will substantially defuse a tense atmosphere. Before finishing, you should ensure that the student (in particular) is clear about how exactly he needs to modify his behaviour to prevent future problems. If you believe it is the teacher who is at fault, it would be sensible to discuss the matter with the Head Teacher in case any disciplinary action is necessary.

Disputes among students, staff and parents

My personal experience is that most meetings involving students, staff and parents at least end up on a positive note, provided that the student is involved in the process. In the final analysis, the only way in which a student's behaviour will improve is if the student perceives that her or his actions or attitude are at least contributing to a problem, and s/he then decides to do something about it.

This is more likely to happen when the student has been in a meeting where s/he can make a contribution and, equally, can be challenged on particular inaccuracies which may have crept in when the student initially reported a situation to parents. If the parents see that you have actually investigated the incidents and can corroborate what you say from the mouth of the student, then they are more likely to support you. If you anticipate that the parent may not be helpful – possibly believing a false denial by the student – it is wise to have taken statements from other students, which you can then quote without necessarily naming your sources. This shows that you have made a detailed investigation.

Exclusion meetings

As a deputy head you may have to take part in an exclusion meeting, where the question of readmission of a student is being considered. Such meetings will usually include at least a governor, a representative of the local education authority, one or more member of staff, the student's parents and the student. I do not propose to deal in detail with these here since local practices vary greatly.

Nevertheless, I would make two points: first, you ought not to be asked to act for the head in such a meeting without having sat in on one previously; and, secondly, the quasi-legal nature of such meetings will be very apparent when you do take part in one.

POINTS TO NOTE

- [ ] Schools exist for students.
- [ ] All deputies have a pastoral role.
- [ ] The tutor is a key person in the pastoral system.
- [ ] Reward and recognition creates the right atmosphere.
- [ ] Sanctions should be clear and demonstrably fair.
- [ ] Parents should be kept informed.
- [ ] Remember 'natural justice'.
- [ ] You may be required to deal with the extra-difficult situations that arise.

4

BEYOND THE WALLS

Civility costs nothing and buys everything
(Lady Montagu)

One area where you are likely to find yourself acting for the head very quickly is in dealing with telephone calls and visitors to the school. These calls or visits are likely to come either from parents (or prospective parents) or from members of the public. How you deal with these unscheduled contacts may have a disproportionate effect on the school's reputation, and possibly even on its ongoing viability.

You need to give careful thought to how you will handle such opportunities to enhance the school's image. The use of the word 'opportunities' is deliberate, because it is only by viewing each contact as such that a school will be able to turn what may be a potential drawback into what they would call in business a 'winning advantage'. It is much easier to do this if the school has an open-door (and telephone) policy, which aims to deal with any query or complaint quickly and effectively and starts with how the telephone is answered or how the visitor is greeted. It is useful to look at each medium for communication in turn.

DEALING WITH TELEPHONE CALLS

Think back to the last time you wanted to buy something – whether it was car insurance or a new washing machine – and you had to make a few telephone enquiries; or think of the last time you tried to make a complaint by telephone. How was the initial call answered? Did the person you spoke to sound helpful and sympathetic? Did she speak as if the future of the firm mattered to her, or did she try to suggest that it was nothing at all to do with her?

Now think of the last time you rang a school. What was the initial response? Did it sound like the kind of place you would like to work in or send a child to? Did you get an effective answer to your query? If the person you wished to speak to was unavailable, was your message passed on and your call returned? Have you rung your own school recently? Did the way the telephone was answered make you proud you worked there – or did it embarrass you?

You will immediately say that you are not the person who answers the telephone. But you are a senior manager. If you feel that the school is not handling this aspect of its communication process properly, then you need to draw attention to it. It may well require some considerable tact – you do not want to upset the head's personal secretary if you can avoid it – but nevertheless the point should be made if need be. One way of doing this is for you to answer the telephone yourself if you are in the office and all the lines are ringing at once. You are showing a willingness to help and are hopefully providing a role model. Remember that many people who answer the telephone have never had any training in doing so, because it is only comparatively recently that even the business world has woken up to the importance of initial telephone contacts.

You may well find yourself asked to deal with a caller who has rung demanding that s/he speak to the head. You need to introduce yourself as a deputy head teacher – most callers will accept a deputy head taking such a call – and ask how you can help. Then listen! Note down any points of relevance, such as the caller's name, their place of work, and so on, which are mentioned in the initial comments. If it is a query, either answer the question or promise to get the answer for the caller. Take a telephone number so that you can return the call with the answer when you find it, or tell the caller the name of the person who will ring back with the answer. The caller may be a parent who is worried about a child's progress or whose child has some problem related to school. If the office has tried unsuccessfully to speak to the appropriate head of house/year, tutor or class teacher (in schools where this is normal practice), state that you will pass a message on personally and will ask the appropriate person to ring back. Make sure that s/he does.

If the caller has a complaint, sympathize and indicate that you want to help. It is quite likely that the person concerned is very annoyed and it may not be the first time that something has happened to cause such annoyance. Offer to take realistic action and make sure that you have a contact number. Then make a note in your diary to ring back in a few days' time to check if the caller is happier about the situation. Progress the matter in stages as necessary until it is resolved.

Above all, treat every person in the same way. Speak to everyone as if s/he has four highly motivated children all waiting to enrol at your school in return for some helpful answers! Deal with the query/problem/complaint as efficiently and effectively as possible. Keep calm and sound as though you know the answer – even when you are not too sure yourself!

UNANNOUNCED VISITORS

The same general rules as above apply to how you deal with unannounced visitors, except that you may be faced with someone who is going to refuse to move from the school unless the problem is sorted out there and then.

The first thing is to greet the person self-confidently and offer a handshake. Some schools have a reception area where you can talk to visitors, failing which you will probably have to see them in your office. Offer the visitor a seat and then ask how you can help. Follow the guidelines suggested for the telephone call: listen, sympathize, outline realistic action. Promise to investigate the matter and to telephone or write in response. A further meeting might be suggested after you have had time to carry out your promise.

When you need the meeting to come to an end – it may have become an unproductive exercise in repetition – you can either indicate this by standing up and thanking the person for coming in, or it might be wise in some cases to arrange for the office to ring you, thus giving the opportunity to end the meeting.

There may be times when you feel personally threatened, in which case you should let the office know that you would like an additional colleague present. There should be a school procedure for such eventualities: more than one school has had a visitor who is the worse for drink or drugs.

Most contacts with people outside the school will nevertheless be planned. You obviously have more control over these than with the unannounced visits dealt with above, and in many cases the initiative for the contact will come from you. There are many different categories of people with whom you will have dealings, but in all cases it is important to remember that you are helping to project the image of the school.

CORPORATE CONTACT WITH PARENTS

Parents meetings

Many parents were educated in an age when their parents were not welcome, never mind welcomed, in school unless they were sent for – and that usually meant trouble! Nowadays schools do accept the rights of parents to know what is going on, and most schools try to involve parents positively in the educational process. It is important to remember that they may still find school a forbidding place: unpleasant experiences during their own schooldays may make it difficult to go into a school without feeling some sense of trepidation.

The onus is firmly on the school to help break down these barriers. We have already seen how a deputy head will often come into contact with parents. In addition, the organization of more formal parents' evenings, open evenings, careers' conventions, and so on, may come within your job description. If this is the case, then you need to ensure that the aims of the particular event are kept very firmly in focus: in most cases, you want to encourage the maximum number to attend and you want them to feel it has been worthwhile.

Encouraging maximum attendance starts with your initial contact, which is usually via a letter sent home with the students. (Sometimes a school publishes dates of such events in advance, in which case the letter will be the second point of contact.) The letter needs to sound welcoming, to be written in simple English, and to set out all the necessary information clearly, particularly the date(s) and timing(s). The use of a reply slip is recommended, so as to act as some kind of check on 'student post'; in some cases it may be desirable to send a personal invitation through the post in the case of particular students.

The next thing is to check that the buildings have been booked and that the caretaker knows what rooms, furniture and so on will be needed. Relevant ancillaries need to know this not just to get things in the right place but also in some cases to rearrange cleaning schedules. Decisions need to be taken on the timings of evenings and – particularly, but not exclusively, in the case of secondary schools – whether or not an appointments' system should be used. Parents should be involved in such decisions, although you must be realistic in that you may not get a clear answer to your enquiries in every case.

You may be responsible also for the detailed organization of the evening itself. The first question you should ask yourself is, 'Is it obvious which entrance should be used?' If you are not sure, try going out of the school grounds and then actually walking back in as if you were a stranger. If it is not absolutely clear where such a visitor should go, then get some signs put up. Make sure that the signs inside the building are also clear to strangers.

Staff should have name badges for special events involving parents, in such a form and shape that they can be easily read, and saying what their wearer's function is (for example, 'Jane Brown, English teacher'). If the parents are likely to have to wait to see a particular teacher, then make sure that there are seats for them. Try to anticipate the flow of people through and around the site, and use students to escort parents where possible (and remember to get parental permission slips signed for such students and the need for them to get home safely afterwards).

Some kind of refreshment should be provided, both for staff and for parents. Again, this is an area where students are usually more than willing to be involved, and one that allows them to act as school ambassadors. The Parent–Teacher Association is usually also more than willing to help.

Check over things on the day itself. If something is not right, get it put right. Above all, keep calm!

Off-site activities

You should also consider how contact may be made with parents off the school premises. Some schools run 'surgeries' from time to time in different locations in the community – for example, in a local library or community centre – and for many parents these can be easier to get to and seem less threatening. Some secondary schools find that having meetings in a primary school can also be easier for some parents.

The Parent Teacher Association

The role and nature of Parent–Teacher Associations (PTAs) has been redefined as a result of the education legislation of the 1980s and its effect on the structure of school governing bodies; indeed, many parents who were once active in the PTA are now on the governing body itself. However, there are still parents – as well as parents of former students, and other members of the local community – who want to be involved in the school without committing themselves to the range of responsibilities inherent in becoming a school governor.

In most schools the head attends the PTA meetings, and it may fall to one or more of the deputies to do so as well. You should resist the temptation to look on the PTA primarily as a source of extra money; there are many more useful things that they can do to enhance the school, not least by acting as ambassadors. If they are willing to be involved in helping with the curriculum or with parents' evenings, this can be very beneficial.

Some schools have a 'Friends of ...' organization, which functions like a PTA but which has the advantage of attracting support and help from other members of the community who may not have children at the school.

CONTACT WITH SCHOOL GOVERNORS

In some schools, deputies are invited to meetings of the governing body, either for specific items where they can offer expertise, or on a rotational basis with the other deputies, or as a matter of course as members of the senior management team. If you are considering headship in the future, it is essential that you attend governors' meetings. If you do not do so, you will find it increasingly difficult to deal with interviews for head teacher posts, which increasingly assume such attendance.

It is important to remember that school governors take on very many responsibilities very quickly, and that not all have been trained adequately for them. Even where there has been adequate training, it is still important to remember that they may have little experience of the curriculum, of school budgeting, or of the many legal aspects of being a governor. They will almost invariably be doing the job in their spare time and may indeed have come to a meeting following a day's work. Your responses to questions will have to avoid sounding patronizing on the one hand or being incomprehensible on the other.

In the final analysis, it is also important to remember that the governors have a vote and you do not (unless you are a staff governor). They have significant powers, the exercise of which can have a great effect on how the school operates. Your advice needs to be coherent and reasoned if you wish them to heed it.

LINKS WITH OTHER EDUCATIONAL ESTABLISHMENTS: CURRICULAR CONTINUITY

The issue of curricular continuity between one phase of education and the next is crucial to the progress of students. Whether you teach in a primary school whose students go to several secondary schools, a secondary school with several 'feeder' primary schools or a sixth-form/tertiary college drawing students from a wide range of secondary schools, you may be given the specific responsibility of organizing such links.

If you are responsible for this, you need to remember that the main purpose of such links is to improve the learning process for the students. It thus follows that the relationships should not be based on the premise that the most important thing is to maximize numbers for one institution or another. (You cannot, of course, ignore this, but virtue usually has its own reward.) There should instead be serious attempts to ascertain what students have been doing in their previous schools, where they are in terms of academic achievement, and how your institution can best provide for them if they – and/or their parents – choose that they go there. The information (including records of achievement) that your students are to take with them needs to be carefully selected.

As the secondary school deputy head in charge of such liaison you should encourage primary-school class teachers (particularly, but not exclusively, Year 6 teachers) or departmental heads to become involved in the process. Proper information systems need to be established, and you have a key role in this. It also needs to be agreed how best to transfer SAT and GCSE results.

CONTACT IN THE LOCAL COMMUNITY

The relationship between the school and the community is worthy of at least one book in itself. Here I offer a few thoughts on where this has particular significance for the deputy head teacher.

We have already looked above at the possibility of contact being made with the school via the telephone or by personal visit. Such contacts are more likely to be for the purpose of complaining than anything else. The sensible school takes steps to initiate contact with the community before such complaints occur. Each school has a different situation and therefore different opportunities, but the important thing is that the intention exists to establish meaningful contact and relationships with the local community.

The idea of community service is well established in many places, and where this is so it is important that senior staff actually visit students when they are engaged in this work. It is important that you remember that you carry a certain status within the community as a deputy head.

You may also be given responsibility for community links. The first thing is to make contact with those people in the community who already have a relationship with the school, and to introduce yourself to them. The facilities of the school – such as being able easily to contact parents or to photocopy communications – may be attractive to community groups. Make sure that community links are formalized in some way so that there is a forum established for considering how effective the links are and how they may be further developed. For some communities, the school is their biggest investment and has the best buildings; the school may also be the major employer in the area.

It is important to remember that while some parents may be represented in such community forums, many of them will not, and so a community forum is not a replacement for specific contact with parents.

Evening centres and youth clubs

There may be an adult evening centre attached to the school and, again, you may be the nominated school representative to maintain effective links. There will be occasions where day and evening activities may result in some friction between some of the school staff and the evening-centre staff.

Your job as deputy head teacher of the school is to put forward the school's perspective, while at the same time recognizing that only the exercise of goodwill on both sides will enable the community to gain maximum benefit from their facility. Progress is best made if an attempt is made to focus on facts, rather than engaging in a meaningless debate on whose rights should carry most weight.

Remember also that there is a good chance that at least some of the governing body of your school may be involved in the running of the evening centre as well, and their assistance should not be overlooked in trying to solve what can sometimes appear to be a tricky problem.

Much the same applies to youth clubs. One particular problem that can arise is where a student has been excluded from school but attends the youth club. This is an example of where a good working relationship between yourself and the person in charge of the youth club can be helpful.

Involvement with local businesses

Links with the local business community can be of benefit to both parties, provided that the atmosphere is the right one. If the school merely views business as a way of getting donations for a minibus and the business community is merely looking for cheap labour, then any links are bound to founder fairly quickly. On the other hand, we all have a vested interest in producing a well trained and educated local population for the future. If schools and local businesses can work together with this in view, the beneficiaries will be both the young people and the firms involved.

One very useful initiative that you can encourage is the Teacher Placement service, which aims to put teachers into industry and vice versa. The importance of this is that it is a first step towards establishing relationships based on knowledge of how business operates and how schools operate. Very often teachers' knowledge about industry and commerce – and vice versa – is inaccurate, particularly with so many teachers having gone straight from higher education back into schools and with many industrialists thinking that schools have not changed since they were educated. Establishing facts is a necessary prerequisite of combating such prejudice. Through the Teacher Placement Service, both sides have the opportunity to see how the other works. Remember, though, that in the same way that no school is truly typical, you are also unlikely to find a truly typical business. It goes without saying that your approach to establishing links should be based on a feeling of mutual respect for the perspective of the other.

For deputy heads in particular, involvement in part of the management training programme of a local firm can be very helpful. In your senior management position and with such a placement, you will be able to see how others manage in a different environment. Sometimes the absence of other educationalists can be especially helpful in enabling you to take a completely fresh look at how you do your job. You may have to think and make the connections for yourself, but thinking does no lasting harm!

POINTS TO NOTE

❑ Civility costs nothing.
❑ The telephone is a powerful image-builder.
❑ Complaints present opportunities.
❑ Schools must seek to involve parents.
❑ Governors need sound professional advice to do their job well.
❑ The school belongs to the community.
❑ Schools should build links with local businesses.
❑ The Teacher Placement Service provides useful management training.

5

CURRICULUM AND TIMETABLE

Progress ... is not an accident but a necessity
(Herbert Spencer)

One could argue that the curriculum provides the *raison d'être* of any school. The nature of the curriculum is therefore quite rightly the subject of much debate and there are many views both on its content and on its delivery. This chapter does not propose to look at the philosophical arguments surrounding the topic but rather to consider the management role of the deputy head in curriculum planning and delivery. For the purposes of our analysis, it will be assumed that the responsibility for curriculum planning, evaluation and timetabling is vested in one person, although many schools organize things differently; it should be easy for institutions that share these responsibilities among a group of staff to adapt the detail.

The general argument for a theory of management practice is that it is better to plan outcomes than to wait blissfully and just hope that the outcomes you want will happen. This argument is particularly relevant to this area of school management. Unthinking acceptance of the status quo can result in stagnation. This in turn means that the reason for students being in school is not planned and is therefore only going to be successful by chance rather than by design.

It is partly because of the previously haphazard and inconsistent nature of the curriculum from one part of the country to the other that we now have the National Curriculum, which sets out the broad framework for the curriculum for students up to the age of 16. One result has been that the curriculum for post-16 education has been scrutinized more vigorously so as to try to ensure that there is some logical connection between the National Curriculum and what follows.

A deputy head teacher will need to have clear strategies for getting agreement on the curriculum that is to be offered, for turning it into a practical reality and for producing means of evaluating its effectiveness. Before looking at these management dimensions, it may be helpful to look briefly at the context within which this happens.

THE NATIONAL CURRICULUM

There is little doubt that a central framework for the curriculum – embodied in the Education Reform Act 1988 – will remain. There have been several major revisions of the National Curriculum since it was introduced, and it is important to keep up to date with the latest (legal) requirements. We shall look at a few key points in the course of this chapter.

One other change that the National Curriculum certainly brought to education was the introduction of a new terminology with which it is necessary to be familiar: such phrases as 'key stages', 'core subjects', 'foundation subjects', 'attainment targets', 'programmes of study', SATs, etc. A short summary of the meaning of each is given below (as applicable to schools in England and Wales; requirements in Scotland and Northern Ireland are different).

Key stages

The years of compulsory schooling (5–16) are divided into four key stages, and the old way of naming school years has been changed. Table 5.1 sets these out. One result of this is that the term 'seventh-year students' may mean 18-year-olds to one member of staff and 11-year-olds to another in an 11–18-year-range school. Some interesting conversations can ensue!

Table 5.1 *Key stages*

KEY STAGE	DESCRIPTION	PUPILS' AGE AT END OF SCHOOL YEAR
1	Year 1	6
	Year 2	7
2	Year 3	8
	Year 4	9
	Year 5	10
	Year 6	11
3	Year 7	12
	Year 8	13
	Year 9	14
4	Year 10	15
	Year 11	16

Table 5.2 *Core and foundation subjects*

CORE SUBJECTS	FOUNDATION SUBJECTS
English	History
Mathematics	Geography
Science	Technology (including design)
	Information Technology
	Modern foreign language
	Key stages 3 and 4:
	Music
	Art
	PE

Core and foundation subjects

Certain subjects must now, by law, be on the curriculum of all students between the ages of 5 and 16 in maintained schools. These are set out in Table 5.2.

Welsh is also compulsory in schools in Wales. The Secretary of State at the Department for Education and Employment (DfEE) has eased the requirement to study any foundation subjects at Key Stage 4. It is compulsory at this key stage to take English, Mathematics, Science, Technology and a modern foreign language. In addition, students have to study History or Geography. Art and Music will be optional; PE may be optional. Secondary schools are, at the time of writing (1998), able to drop the requirements at Key Stage 4 for Science, Technology and a modern foreign language in certain circumstances. At Key Stage 1 and Key Stage 2, the programmes of study have been severely curtailed, in order to give added time and emphasis to the development of literacy and numeracy.

While every school has to make provision for religious education, parents do have the right to ask for their children to be exempted from it. This can lead to some problems where RE is part of an integrated humanities course. It can also cause interesting anomalies between sixth-form colleges (which are subject to school regulations) and tertiary and other further education colleges (which are not).

Although the core and foundation subjects must be taught, they can be combined or taught under other names, provided that the prescribed content is covered. Such content used to be known as 'a syllabus' but is now referred to in new ways (see next subsection hereunder).

Attainment targets and programmes of study

Each subject has prescribed 'attainment targets', and these set out the knowledge and skills that students should have at the different stages of schooling between the ages of 5 and 16. These attainment targets are accompanied by 'programmes of study', which describe what students need to be taught to allow them to achieve the prescribed attainment targets. The teaching methods and exact content are left to the school to decide within the programmes of study.

There are eight levels of attainment, with level descriptions, and these set out what students should know at different stages. When we look at evaluation and assessment later in this chapter, we can consider some of the problems raised by these levels of attainment and the reporting requirements associated with them.

Standard Assessment Tasks (SATs)

Assessment is carried out at the end of each of the four key stages by a mixture of teacher assessment and standard assessment tasks (SATs). The results of these are to be used as a record of progress.

BEYOND THE NATIONAL CURRICULUM

While the National Curriculum provides a basic compulsory framework for the curriculum up to the age of 16, it does not as yet extend to students older than that; nor does it inhibit at least some of the innovative ideas in curriculum development and provision that have been a feature of the educational system in the United Kingdom. We will deal with GCSE in more detail later in this chapter, but it should be noted at this point that one of the main effects of this examination system for 16-year-olds has been to put even more pressure on schools to look at their post-16 provision. There has also been an increasing awareness nationally that our system of education and training is lagging far behind other industrialized countries, with very stark economic consequences.

The net effect of all this is that there are few schools nowadays where there are only students in the sixth form who are taking three or more 'A' levels. The deputy head teacher responsible for the curriculum needs to be aware of the trends in this area, including the discussion centring round the provision of a balanced course that includes 'core' skills, not to mention 'A/S' levels, GNVQs, NVQs and other comparable qualifications.

There are real issues to be resolved, including the tension between compulsion within the curriculum (to provide a broadly based core of skills among the adults of the later 1990s, which is perceived to be necessary by many involved in both education and industry) and the tradition of freedom for students to choose a fairly restricted diet of three 'A' levels. We need also to remember that when the issues *are* resolved and the curriculum decided, there is the minor matter of writing a timetable to enable it all to happen – a rock on which more than one ship has perished in the past!

In addition to the subjects in the National Curriculum, there are very important areas of experience that most schools believe should be part of the curriculum of all students. Such cross-curricular issues as personal and social education (PSE), environmental education and an understanding of economics have somehow also to be fitted into the curriculum. The government also increasingly lends its weight to what some may cynically view as 'flavours of the month'; thus schools can also be required to ensure that moral education is taught or that citizenship finds it place in the curriculum.

CURRICULUM REVIEW

A deputy head in a secondary school may find that s/he has been given responsibility for the curriculum and/or timetable. This particular function does not have a direct counterpart in primary schools and therefore much of what follows in this chapter is more relevant to secondary school deputies than primary ones.

When you take on the management of the curriculum for the first time, it is important that you find out the following:

❑   the curriculum that exists in the school;
❑   what the consultation structures are for deciding the nature of the curriculum and its associated assessment procedures;
❑   how the school keeps the effectiveness of the curriculum under constant review.

First steps

Your personal review should start with obtaining and reading any documents that exist. These will include the information provided when you applied for the post (which may or may not tell you a lot), the school brochure, syllabuses/programmes of study of individual departments, and such booklets as are prepared for parents at Key Stages 1, 2 or 3 and for students at Key Stage 4 and post-16 levels. These documents will form part of the basis for the next stage of your review, and your knowledge of them will indicate to your colleagues that you have taken some care to find out what the school is about, at least in official literature.

Your next step should be to arrange individual meetings with the head teacher and heads of department/faculty, with a clear agenda of ascertaining present practice. Ask questions and seek clarification, but try to resist giving all your revolutionary ideas to them at this stage: just because the ideas impressed the interviewing panel, it does not mean that they are automatically right (or, for that matter, wrong). You will have some values that you would like to see embodied in the curricular practice of the school, but other people have similar wishes and intentions. The bottom line is that your job is to manage the curriculum and curriculum change, not to impose it by fiat.

By now you will have an official picture of the school's practice in the curriculum and some idea of how consultation is carried on. This, of course, may be a complete myth, and you need to find out what really goes on in practice. This is where you have to be both diplomatic and clear-minded in what you are seeking to find out.

It needs to be said very clearly at this point that much of what has gone under the name of curriculum practice in the past, while well intentioned and noble, has often described what it looked like in theory. For example, many option schemes for GCSE students seem to specify 'breadth' by asking them to choose at least one science subject, one humanities subject, one practical subject and two or three more; but when this is translated into practice, and you actually look at the curriculum of individual students, boys are studying chemistry, physics, geography, geology and technology, while girls in the same school are studying biology, child care, cookery, history and French. The point to be made is that any detailed review of the curriculum needs to look at what the students are actually doing, not just at what the timetable and options booklets suggest they might be doing.

If you approach colleagues in a supportive and positive way, you will almost invariably find that they are quite happy to show you examples of the work of students. You should also be able to see such examples on display in classrooms: regularly walking about the school and observing will give you further opportunities to ascertain what goes on in classrooms.

Forward thinking

Having formed some idea of present practice, you next want to find out how the school should be going forward over the coming years. Disraeli has said: 'Change is inevitable. In a progressive country change is constant.' If this is true, as I believe it to be, then your only choice is whether change will be constant and planned, or disjointed and unplanned. Being a senior manager is tantamount to stating your belief that change can be planned – otherwise why have managers?

You cannot, of course, change everything at once; nor, indeed, should you want to. What you *should* want to do, however, is to ensure that the school evolves with changing circumstances and that structures are created that enable this to happen. The best first step towards getting this accepted as part of the culture, if it does not already exist, is to initiate *some* change, however small.

To find out what needs to be changed, one effective way forward is to arrange to see heads of department again and ask them how they see the curriculum developing over the next few years, particularly (but not exclusively) in their subject. It is worth noting that when you talk about this type of change, it is rare indeed that such change will be confined to a colleague's teaching subject, since almost every curricular change (GCSE being an excellent example of this) has some implications for methodology and for other parts of the curriculum.

You should see your responsibility for curricular review in terms of an annual planning cycle.

THE ANNUAL PLANNING CYCLE

It is important for the school that an annual planning cycle exists and that it starts early enough to allow time to consider possible changes carefully and to make preparation for any that are accepted. The more fundamental the change, the more time needs to be allowed for it to be considered and its implementation planned.

There are some changes that will need more than a year to implement, allowing for full consultation – a change to the school day may be one such change, although recent legislation allows this to happen more quickly than formerly – and in these circumstances planning needs to start at an appropriate stage in the previous year's cycle. The latest time you should start thinking about the school timetable for a particular academic year – which will be the final visible evidence of curriculum planning for that year – is the *previous* September.

Table 5.3 shows a sample timetable suitable for curriculum issues, assuming that an appropriate consultation meeting is held in the school twice a term. If a different consultation cycle operates in your school, then these suggestions will need to be amended to take account of that.

Table 5.3 *Curriculum planning cycle*

MEETING	ACTIVITY	CURRICULUM ISSUES
Autumn-1	Discuss	Proposals for changes to length of lessons within existing school day; courses to be offered 14–16 and post-16.
Autumn-2	Decide	Changes (if any) to length of lessons.
	Discuss	Overall curriculum, including time allocations to subjects.
Spring-1	Decide	Time allocations to individual subjects; courses to be offered 14–16 and post-16.
	Discuss	Likely numbers of classes in each year.
Spring-2	Decide	Numbers of classes in each year.
	Discuss	Likely provision of 'support'.
Summer-1	Report	Any changes in numbers which may affect decisions taken earlier.
Summer-2	Discuss	Agenda for next year's curriculum cycle, including advance notice of any mooted changes.
	Report	Progress of timetable construction

When we look (in Chapter 11) at your personal time management, we shall consider the need for annual planning from your own point of view. Furthermore, in Chapter 10, on meetings, consideration will be given to the whole process of planning. Suffice it to say at this point that a document setting out proposals for discussion should be circulated in advance and should try to anticipate likely points both for and against, in order that an effective discussion can be held and a decision taken. It is as well to be clear in your own mind about the kinds of arguments that are likely to be raised when decisions such as those above are under review. Some possibilities are set out below for the major ones.

Length of lessons

While the possibility of changing the starting/finishing times and/or the length of the school day is a whole-school issue that should involve consultations not only with teaching staff but also with non-teaching staff, bus companies, parents, students, etc, the length of lessons within the existing timings is usually seen as a matter for teaching staff alone. The governors are likely to support any such change, provided that they can be convinced that it makes curricular sense. As the deputy head teacher in charge of curriculum, you may be given the responsibility for chairing discussion of such proposed changes.

There is an almost infinite range of possibilities on this topic. Schools have operated all kinds of systems, such as a two-week cycle, a nine-day cycle, a six-day cycle, a 41-period week, and so on. The fact that no universal system has been adopted suggests that every arrangement has disadvantages, and therefore you will be wise to assume that the best you can hope for is a compromise (more on this below). While many variations are possible, nevertheless most secondary schools operate a 25-, a 30- or a 40-period week; and the longer ones are often operated in 'double' sessions for many subjects, particularly with older students, which can effectively mean that a 40-period week operates for most of the time like a 20-period one.

If a change is suggested, it is important that all views are considered. It is also important that you make clear that you are prepared to implement a change if the staff want it, while at the same time suggesting that a change is not inevitable if there is no clear advantage to be gained by it. Also remember that there are pastoral considerations within such changes, and that there may be a wish to move and/or lengthen/shorten the time given for assemblies and tutorial sessions.

There are several different reasons why the best you can hope for is a compromise, of which the three most significant are the differing needs of subjects, the nature of the learning process, and the physical movement of staff and students around the school.

First of all, some subject areas are best suited to sessions of at least one-and-a-half hours, particularly where practical work is involved. Examples would include subjects that span the traditional design and realization areas and/or home economics. The time spent in changing for PE lessons militates against short lessons, although PE is an example of a subject that needs longer lessons but would ideally benefit from seeing students take part more than once a week if a formal fitness programme has been planned. Modern languages students need regular exposure to the language and it is usually preferable for the students to participate every day for short sessions rather than twice a week for longer ones.

The age of the students is also a significant factor. While staff may have one view on how long younger students can concentrate, they may wish for the continuity of longer sessions with older students. The learning process suggests that older students need at least an hour to become really fully productive and therefore 35- or 40-minute lessons are not very effective. If one timetable is to be operated for students of varying ages, compromises will have to be made here.

A third point to be considered is physical movement round the school. The fewer the lessons, the fewer times students will be moving from one place to another. Apart from the waste of time – which may not in fact be such a problem since a break and a change of air can be beneficial to the learning process – a high degree of movement about the school offers lots of opportunities for accidents and altercations. Most schools probably find that the amount of hassle during lessons is minimal compared with that generated in corridors and playgrounds.

An understandable reaction when considering these options is to assume that since there is no ideal solution, it is not worth even debating the issue of lesson length. However, even if change does not result, it is important that staff have the opportunity to consider the issue, if only to indicate that their views are valued. It is very easy to assume that because you have spent some time – possibly in a previous school – debating the issue, then everyone has, or indeed that the answer obtained previously was right for all time and for all places.

My personal experience suggests that a school where such issues are considered from time to time, and where the views of all staff are sought, will have a positive atmosphere. At all costs avoid such clichés as, 'I thought we settled this in 1992!' and 'There's nothing new in education.' Remember also that the member of staff who prefaces his remarks with, 'With all due deference …', has no intention of deferring to anyone, whether senior management or otherwise. Tired clichés betray tired minds; and tired minds are not much use in a dynamic, learning-focused school.

Courses to be offered

Your initial aim for developing any new courses should be to move steadily from the present to the future. There may occasionally be a case for a 'root and branch' approach to the whole curriculum, but this should be seen as a major undertaking and the new millennium may not be the most auspicious time for such surgery, in view of the volume and speed of change of the last two decades. In any case, we have already suggested that a school should be in a process of continual but gradual change, which is more effective than stagnation followed by revolution.

There are innovations in course development that are limited to one department (in so far as any change in the curriculum does not impinge in some way on others) and that are therefore usually the subject of debate within that one subject area. You should be kept aware of such possibilities, partly so that you can give relevant advice and partly so that you can take account of any wider implications (eg for staffing, training, finance).

It is a good idea if departments at least report such developments to the rest of the staff through the normal channels of communication.

Where a change impinges directly upon more than one department, your role is very important. An example would be the introduction of a GNVQ programme for the 14–16 age range. A commitment will be needed from several subject areas if such a proposal is to be accepted, and it will have wide implications for any options scheme on offer.

You need to focus the minds of all concerned on very specific questions, such as the following. Is there an awareness of the time and training needed? Is there a long-term commitment to it? Does it depend too much on one member of staff, whose departure would leave everyone else in the mire? Will the students benefit? Who will pay for it? Have all the departments taken the innovation on board, and are they prepared to make it a priority? By raising these questions, you are performing a vital role if the new course is to start off with realistic, attainable targets. Given positive responses, there is a good chance of success. Remember to build in specific review meetings for at least the first year or two until the innovation becomes a natural part of course provision.

Time allocation

With the National Curriculum, there is less and less scope for altering the balance of time allocated to different subjects. Thus the proposals you present at an appropriate consultation meeting may not differ greatly from those of the previous year. There is still scope, however, for some movement (for example, an increase of one period for maths in Year 7) provided that you remember that (assuming no overall extension of the learning week) an increase for one subject will mean a loss for another. Sometimes this will be readily agreed by all concerned, although most heads of department are aware these days of the staffing and financial implications of agreeing to a loss of curriculum time for their subject and thus may not be ready to agree willingly to any such loss.

There is still the scope – some would argue it as a necessity – for subjects working together to deliver overlapping attainment targets. Where this occurs, it is likely that the implications will be more readily observed when you come to preparing the timetable than at this stage.

A more fundamental review of time allocations – as opposed to minor changes here and there – needs to be planned more than a year in advance and needs a wider consultation process than the usual half-termly committee. Appendix 1 gives an example of how one school approached such a review.

How many classes?

It is now accepted in many secondary schools that the decision on how many classes there should be in each year group is a matter that should at least be reported to heads of department through the usual consultation procedures. Although support, blocking, and so on can present a rather diverse picture on the school timetable, the basic building block is still the class.

Let us suppose that you expect to have 120 students in Year 9. This can be organized in a variety of ways: a few examples are four classes of 30, five classes of 24, a 'top' class of 28 with four more classes of 23, or even six classes of 20. You need to ascertain which options the school can afford, and this means getting some indication from the governors on likely affordable staffing levels for the next year. With LMS and the restricted budgets of the past number of years, you may not get this decision until the last minute in the fiscal year (ie 1 April or later), which will shorten the period available for preparing your timetable.

Another factor that can be a major annual problem for some schools is that you may have to make a very rough guess as to your intake, and yet this estimate can be crucial to your work on the curriculum. If you estimate an intake of 155 and plan six classes, including a special needs group, you only need to get a variation of ten students to put real pressure on the timetable – a lower number will have financial (and therefore staffing) implications for future years, but a sudden increase in numbers in September is the more immediate problem.

Expectations of class size may differ from one department to another – for example, there may be a written (or unwritten) rule that workshop classes will be limited to a maximum of 25. If your school operates a policy like this, it has implications for how many classes you can operate. On our previous example, if you have planned five workshop classes of 24 (for a total of 120 students) and your intake increases to 126, you have a problem. Some schools are dealing with this by assuming the highest number and accepting smaller classes in the intake year if this number turns out to be optimistic. The difficulty with this approach is that not only is there a future financial (and staffing) implication but that it may mean larger classes further up the school; it may also mean reorganizing the intake year into a smaller number of classes in the next year, with the consequent disruption this will cause to class atmosphere and staffing.

The provision of support

Decisions need to be taken on 'support', whether for students with special needs or for departments. The provision of support has the advantage of giving some flexibility to deal with any timetabling difficulties that may appear. You should ask heads of department to prioritize their requests, and you should try to be even-handed in allocating teacher support (as opposed to student support, where the subject with the students needing support gets it automatically by virtue of having the students).

Do not make promises you cannot keep. It is much better, from a psychological point of view, to be cautious about the possibilities of support rather than to raise expectations only then to disappoint. Try to think about the issue from the point of view of the teacher in the classroom. Most of us anticipate what we will be doing next year – sometimes as an antidote to what is happening this year; furthermore, much of teaching is a psychological state rather than a physical one – you only have to look at the different sizes of classes throughout the country and how staff feel about these to confirm this view. If a teacher thinks he or she is going to be provided with support for (say) year-10 GCSE students and then does not get it, that teacher is going to feel at least a little demoralized, since s/he may have planned some ways of improving the teaching (say, for example, in the area of oral work) using the support offered. If a teacher in those circumstances had not had his or her hopes raised, disappointment might not have set in.

One further point to be made at this point is that the policy for support should be openly publicized in order to stifle any complaints between departments that there is favouritism at work, which is a real danger with some deputy head teachers who have run a department in their own subject for some years. At least a public policy can be questioned and answers can be given: if the answers are reasonable, then you have nothing to worry about. You should also make clear whether or not support will be 'covered' in the event of staff absence. For example, you may provide IT support for English staff with Year 7 classes; if the IT teacher is absent, will someone be expected to fill the gap, and will the same apply if the English teacher is absent? If these issues are discussed, and the rationale for decisions is formulated and explained, then they are less likely to distract staff from their real job of helping students to learn.

Decision making

It is implicit in most of this chapter that decisions must be taken. It is probably worth stating this explicitly at this point. The school timetable will never appear if senior management is not willing to take decisions, following reasonable and ordered consultation. Hence the need, emphasized here, for planning and the curriculum cycle.

WRITING THE TIMETABLE

The task of the secondary school timetabler is simple: to produce a timetable that allows the curricular aims of the school to be implemented in practice. Just because it is simple, however, does not mean it is easy! The objective of this part of the chapter is to help demystify the process and, I hope, to provide some practical advice that will enable you to produce a timetable that, while not perfect, will at least look like a reasonable attempt at perfection.

Although this section of the book is detailed, it is not a substitute for either working with the timetabler in a school or going on a timetabling course before taking up your deputy headship. Sitting down on your own to do your first timetable is likely to be a daunting prospect – and a disaster for the school – if you rely solely on theory.

The thinking process

Before you sit down – probably in May or June – to begin to write the timetable for the next academic year, you need to have given thought to the parameters within which you will be working. This should always be present in the back of your mind when debates are held about the shape of the curriculum, since every decision will have some implications for the timetable. You should not use the difficulties of writing a timetable as a reason for preventing any curricular change – if you do not want to cope with these challenges, then you should give the job to someone else – but you will need at times to point out some practical implications that others may not have realized. An example of this will help to make the point clear, but first it may be useful to look at some definitions of the terminology used in this section:

❏ *Blocking*: putting all classes in a year group together for a particular subject or group of subjects.
❏ *Banding*: dividing a year group into two sections (each with two or more classes) for a subject or group of subjects.
❏ *Streaming*: organizing a year group into classes based on ability.
❏ *Setting*: streaming a group of classes within a block or band – this would be done by the subject departmental head or by putting one subject (eg English) on at the same time as another (eg Physics).
❏ *Support*: adding an extra teacher or teachers to a class or group of classes, over the normal agreed number – this may be used in some cases to 'withdraw' students for extra help.

Now we can look at our example. Let us take a situation where a consultative group of staff has formed the view that Year 7 pupils – the intake year – would find it easier to settle into school if they had fewer teachers teaching them. Thus they have formed a proposal for volunteer teachers to take a class for a group of related subjects (eg Science/Maths, English/Humanities/PSE). The volunteers already exist and heads of department are favourably disposed towards the idea, being prepared to undertake the in-service training necessary for the staff concerned who are going to be teaching 'outside' their traditional subject area.

It is at this stage that it has to be pointed out that it is traditional in the school – a tradition much valued by departments – that classes are 'blocked' across year groups for most subjects after Year 7. The teachers who are going to teach Year 7 under the new proposal would also be required to teach in each of the other year groups. This might be achieved by 'banding' year groups rather than by 'blocking' them, but departments have indicated that they would not want this. The basic fact, however, is that the proposal for teachers to take a class for a group of related subjects could not be done without departments giving up other things, such as blocking across whole year groups.

Having presented this difficulty, however, it is important that the ultimate decision is left with the staff consultative committee. In the event, in our particular example it was decided to shelve the proposal, not least on account of the arrival of GCSE and National Curriculum.

It is important to note that a proposal for change, although rejected after review and consultation, could well be raised again in the future and the decision may then be different. The point to be made is that the timetabler is providing expertise, not making the decision.

It may seem that you have to walk an impossible tightrope: you need to be accommodating and to encourage curriculum progress, while at the same time you know that you have to write a timetable at the end of all the decision making. It is an important principle that the timetable must serve the curriculum, not the other way round. If in doubt, this is the way you should incline. Just remember, though, that there are limits to what can be achieved on any timetable.

Prioritizing

If you want to write a reasonable timetable you cannot avoid prioritizing. Not every request, however reasonable or desirable, can be met. There are two levels at which you should be doing this ordering of priorities: at whole-school level and at departmental/faculty level.

When you sit down to write the timetable you have to start somewhere. This may seem obvious, even trite, but it can be the source of much confusion, because the point at which you start begins to determine where you are going to end.

Most timetablers start with the oldest age group first, since this is often the most difficult to accommodate. Once you have put year-13 'A' level English with Ms Jones on the timetable for lessons 1 and 2 on Monday morning, for instance, you will not be able to use any blocking that includes this particular teacher. If English is set against Physics with Mr Frier – a not unlikely scenario – then you will not be able to use any blocking which includes that particular teacher either. It is not impossible that as a result of this simple first step, you will not be able to assign Years 10, 11 and 12 for either English or Science. Already you have limited your room for manoeuvre.

When you hear complaints (which you may even have made yourself in the past) that 'the tail is wagging the dog' or that 'the whole school is sacrificed (a nice emotive word!) to the sixth form', just remember that you have got to start somewhere: trite but true! Try to resist the temptation of offering any complainant the opportunity to write the timetable to 'see if you can do it any better'. *You* are being paid to take the decisions and there is always the danger, albeit slight, that the other person will take you up on the offer!

Recording departmental priorities

In addition to setting your priorities (of which more anon), it is also a good idea to ask departments to set *their* priorities. The more you involve the head of each department in deciding which request is most important to that department, the more you will be able to convince the staff in general that you are genuinely attempting to write the best possible timetable.

You are asking for priorities in two areas: first, which staff should teach particular groups and, secondly, which blockings/bandings etc are most important. Figure 5.1 sets out a possible request sheet for such decisions, which you may find useful to use (or adapt) for these initial stages.

You need to fill in the subject name(s) for a department at the top of the sheet. In each year-group box you should indicate the number of groups you expect to operate and for how many periods per week (eg 6 groups for 6 periods). It is useful to total these at the bottom right-hand corner of each box, with a grand total under the 'Year 7' box: this indicates the total number of periods to be covered by the appropriate head of department. If you expect a particular member of staff to cover a particular group, this should also be indicated; otherwise, leave this for the head of department to complete.

TIMETABLE, 1999–2000

SUBJECT(S):
Please indicate your staffing requests below:

SIXTH FORM
YEAR 11
YEAR 10
YEAR 9
YEAR 8
YEAR 7

Staff availability   (Note that _____ periods need to
                                                                  be left within these figures for
____   ____   ____   commitments in other subjects, etc.)

____   ____   ____

____   ____   ____

Please indicate any timetable requests (eg blocking, support) overleaf in order of
priority, and return this form by _____ .

Figure 5.1 *Example of timetable request sheet*

'Staff availability' indicates the total periods to be taught by all staff who are scheduled to teach in the particular subject area. There are two points to be made here. First of all, some staff will teach in more than one subject area, and the number indicated here is the maximum number of periods available to the head of department/faculty concerned. Sometimes you may be approached by a member of staff who wishes to limit, or exclude, his involvement in a particular subject area (eg PE) without necessarily offending the head of department concerned. Your listing of available periods will show this, but you will need to be prepared with some convincing argument about why the name of a particular member of staff is not included in case the head of department approaches you.

Secondly, the total periods available will often be more than those needed to cover the totals indicated in the boxes. That is why you need to make clear that a certain number of periods need to be left for other commitments, and such commitments could include staff development cover, leisure pursuits, and support in other subject areas. It is essential that you make this clear at this particular time. Do not allow heads of department to believe that any extra time will automatically be available for support within their subject area: they may request this but you will make encouraging noises (mistaken for promises) at your peril. As mentioned earlier, never promise what you cannot be certain of delivering. Put the date by which you expect the form to be returned at the bottom and make clear that missing the deadline may prejudice certain requests.

On the reverse of the sheet, departmental requests should be listed in order of priority. Ensure that all requests are clearly written down and make plain that you make no assumptions unless they are listed here. This is particularly important the first time you do the timetable since even your most efficient predecessor (never mind an inefficient one) may have carried some requests around 'in his head', which he has not thought to write down for you. Heads of department will assume that you have been told everything unless you tell them otherwise.

Another advantage of asking for these requests to be written down is that sometimes heads of department are unaware of exactly how much they ask for: if they list twelve requests, and see that they have had nine of them built in to the timetable, this counts as a visibly high rate of success for the timetabler.

Recording whole-school priorities

In addition to these departmental requests, there will also be whole-school priorities, not all of which you would expect to appear on the departmental sheets. Such priorities might include ensuring that the senior management team shares a common non-teaching lesson for a regular meeting, or that there is a spread of relevant staff available for a senior staff rota. You need to gather together a list of all such priorities, plus those requested by departments which may have implications across the timetable.

The following indicates the kind of things that are likely to appear on such a list, with selected examples:

❑   meetings – departmental or senior staff;
❑   room congestion – computer room needed for all Year-7 groups;
❑   departmental conflicts – 'A' level English wants 4 × 2 periods, 'A' level Physics wants (1 × 4) + (2 × 2) periods, but they are set against each other;
❑   staff – one person required to teach 'A' and 'A/S' level in Year 13;
❑   further study – a member of staff attending a BEd course on a certain afternoon each week;
❑   union duties – member of staff with entitlement to a certain day off each week;
❑   off-site activities – an afternoon required for community service for some Year-11 students;
❑   part-timers – Maths teacher on 0.5 wants to work on no more than three days each week and is blocked with Year-10 Maths staff;
❑   blockings – likely to involve most departments with several year groups;
❑   specified times – swimming for Year-7 pupils on a certain lesson each week.

This list should be copied out neatly and kept in front of you at all times. It is easy to forget some of these priorities when you are in the middle of trying to solve a particular timetabling difficulty. The rule is to check, check, check all the time: this is particularly so when you think you have found a breathtakingly simple answer to a thorny problem.

Assessing priorities

Once you have gathered all the request sheets together, the first thing is to take the time to read them all carefully several times, until you know the requests in detail. If you have asked heads of department to spend their time documenting their priorities, the least you owe them is the courtesy of reading what they have provided. You may wish to have a series of formal or informal meetings with individual heads of department, if only to make sure that you understand exactly what they are asking for.

I think it is important to try to get a broad feel of the totality of requests before trying to start the timetable. It is natural to want to get started right away, since you have fairly specific deadlines that must be observed if the school is to have a timetable ready for September: I know of at least one school (not one where I taught) that did not have its timetable until the end of the first week of the Autumn term, which is not a record you should aim to equal! Having said this, it is essential to think before you act, since every action you take on the timetable limits your scope for manoeuvre, in the same way that the opening moves in a game of chess predetermine much of what follows.

Timetabling tools

There are many different ways of writing a timetable – using magnetic boards, pins, coloured pegs, even a computer; interestingly, they all involve at some stage the use of a pencil and a good eraser! The first time you construct a timetable you may have to use the tools already existing at your school, but if you prefer a different approach, do not feel diffident about asking.

A word about the use of a computer may be in order. It is nearly thirty years since I first approached a major company about using a computer to write a timetable, and the issue that was central then is still central: it is possible to program a computer to offer a series of timetabling choices but its effectiveness depends not only on the quality of the software (and particularly on its ability to allow for the uniqueness of the school) but also on the detail provided by the school. Providing such detail can often take up as much time as doing the timetable by hand.

The three advantages that computers can offer are that they can present a range of possibilities to choose from, they can sometimes produce answers that the human brain cannot, and once the information is provided it can be manipulated easily. If you enjoy chess, you will probably eschew the use of the computer and do the work by mental effort alone; if you want a scapegoat, then there is no better one than the school PC.

Two areas in which the computer really comes into its own are, first, checking that you have not allocated one teacher to teach two classes at once and, secondly, printing out endless timetables in all formats (eg teachers, classes, rooms, year groups, individual pupils). Therefore, most timetablers now put the timetable into a computer fairly quickly after completing it.

Making positive progress

Once you have all the information gathered together, the moment of truth arrives when, to return to the analogy of chess, you make your first move.

It is probably best to exercise caution rather than flamboyance at this stage, certainly until you become recognized as one of the great timetablers of all time, at which time you can indulge in your own particular opening gambits!

At this point it is useful to suggest that the first things to go on the timetable are those that are fixed. Examples include agreed sixth-form blockings with other schools, afternoons when a particular year group must be assigned a specific subject, and so on. If something is definite, then write it in in pen; if it is desirable but not absolutely essential, then use pencil.

You can adopt different strategies to get most of the timetable done. Some deputy heads stay at home for a week to work on the problem, and if you adopt this approach you can always use the telephone to carry on any negotiations that become necessary when you realize that there are any particular requests you cannot meet. Other deputies lock their office doors, with perhaps a notice proclaiming, 'Do not disturb except in an emergency – timetabling in progress'.

It is reasonable to expect that you will be able to spend definite chunks of time – say, two hours – making progress with the timetable, but it is also important to take a break from time to time. It is surprising how often the answer to what was becoming an impossible problem suddenly appears when you leave your timetabling board for a while – a walk round the school can restore a proper sense of perspective to what can become a very intense and insular activity.

Sometimes it is worth asking a head of department in with you so as to put a particular difficulty to him or her: s/he will sometimes say that the particular request is not as important as it appears, possibly because some facts have changed. Even if s/he does not say this, sometimes another pair of eyes can help give a different perspective – which may not solve the problem but may suggest an alternative route for you to try.

As a final comment in this section, it seems to me that if constructing a timetable causes a lot of *angst* within you, then it is not for you. If this is so, why hang on to it when others are probably keen to do it? Only if you enjoy doing it is it worthwhile.

The curiosity of others

A strange phenomenon occurs in most schools at timetabling time every year, when the deputy head responsible for it finds it difficult to get on with the timetable because of the increased number of interruptions, with questions and requests from staff who normally exercise their management responsibilities without constant reference to you. Do not be surprised if they seem not to listen to your answers, glance towards the embryonic timetable, or even ask, 'Well, how's it coming on, then?'

It is perfectly natural to want to know what next year's timetable will be, particularly since it can make such a difference to a teacher's working life for a whole year. We all know which class we do not want last lesson on Thursday, and heads of department know which bits of a timetable are going to cause problems within their departments. In an earlier book of mine, *Middle Managers in Schools and Colleges* (Kogan Page, 1990), I stated my advice to heads of department: 'My compromise as a timetabler is to let people look at the timetable if they wish, but warn them that it might change. If a head of department passes on information to his department about an unfinished timetable, which then changes, this forms a very important part of their management training.' On reflection, I would change 'might change' to 'almost certainly will change'.

Publishing the draft timetable

Before you let staff look at the first draft of the timetable, you need to run certain elementary checks on it. Make sure that fixed blocks have been assigned. Use your list of priorities and see how many of them have been satisfied, if only so that you can answer any criticism of failing to meet one by pointing out that you did meet nine others! Look in particular for any major errors, such as timetabling two classes for one room (usually solvable) or two classes at the same time for the same teacher (not so easy!).

The only part of writing the timetable that causes a timetabler any anxiety is when he or she first puts the draft on the staff room noticeboard. No matter how many times you check the contents, there is still the possibility that you have made a mistake, and this is why you write, 'DRAFT', in very large letters on this first copy. You should also instruct staff not to copy it out or photocopy it, since it may (will?) change. Most staff will accept this injunction if you can promise that they will have a copy of the actual timetable very soon. Ask each head of department to check his/her portion and inform you urgently of any errors spotted.

If a mistake is reported to you, do not assume that it is indeed a mistake until you have checked it out yourself. Even if it is an error, do not panic. (Panic is a natural response to a life-threatening situation – which making a serious mistake on the timetable might well turn out to be, but panic rarely helps avoidance of the impending disaster!) Go back to your board and look for a solution. The fact that every school in the country has a timetable every year – even if some of them are less than brilliant –

is living proof that there are solutions. You will be very unlucky indeed if you turn out to be the first deputy head who failed to make at least some kind of timetable work.

There may also be some minor changes suggested by a department that will not affect the timetable in a major way but will make life better for them. If you can make such changes, even at this stage, there is no reason not to do so. However, make sure that you transfer the changes to every copy you have, whether it be for staff or students.

Once the timetable has been checked, and amended as necessary into a final workable version, you should aim to get it copied to staff as quickly as possible so that they can do any forward planning they wish to do. Once you have given it out, resist the temptation to do any more work on it to see if you can make it better. Leave that for next year.

POINTS TO NOTE

❏ The curriculum is the *raison d'être* of the school.
❏ Curriculum review should be continual.
❏ Planning cycles are essential management tools.
❏ The student's curriculum is the real curriculum.
❏ The timetable should serve the curriculum, not the other way round.
❏ Always prioritize requests.
❏ Only make promises you believe you can keep.

6

ASSESSMENT AND EXAMINATIONS

[He] knows the price of everything and the value of nothing
(Oscar Wilde)

The late Sir Alec Clegg (of West Riding, Yorkshire, education fame) once spoke of examinations in this country as 'a vast malevolent industry' – and this was long before SATs. Many are familiar with Oscar Wilde's description of the cynic quoted at the head of this chapter. If cynics are not to rule the educational world, then those who organize assessment and examinations have a heavy weight of responsibility to bear. In this chapter, we shall first of all look at some basic principles and then at practical details for those who have whole-school responsibility for this key management task.

PRINCIPLES AND PURPOSES

Before organizing assessment systems, including examinations and Records of Achievement, it is important to look at the reasons why some at least are needed in schools. Assessment has always been a fundamental issue, although for much of the time it was not addressed – probably because a tacit working agreement had grown up over the years that satisfied most of those with an interest in the outcomes of the educational system. One positive effect of the whole quagmire created by the Education Reform Act 1988 is that the subject of student assessment is now explicit, and can be summed up in the recent cry of many teachers, 'Are we supposed to teach or to test?'

This puts the issue at its starkest, and is to some extent an oversimplification: all teaching involves some assessment, if only to ensure that future teaching is more effective. However, there is little doubt that there comes a point at which additional testing detracts from the learning situation; and this is the point that many think we are now in danger of reaching. Precious teaching time is viewed as being spent on testing students, which should properly be spent on helping them to learn. And not only is the teaching resource considered to be spent in an unwise balance, but –

and this is just one example – the actual entry fees for GCSE can even exceed the total spent in both Years 10 and 11 on books, materials and stationery in preparing students for these examinations.

This book is not the place to delve into the background to this situation, but it is important that key principles are established first and methods of assessment are then put in place that follow these principles. I set some of these out below.

Reasons for assessment

There are different reasons why assessment takes place in schools. First, it is important to know at particular times where a student's strengths and weaknesses lie, in order that his learning can be better organized to develop his potential. This assessment can be of a general nature (eg reading level) or something more specific (eg the ability to carry out simple multiplication exercises in maths), but the outcome of measuring the level of achievement should be to ensure that the student's performance improves as a result. Secondly, the aggregation of test results can give a class teacher important information on both individuals and on the class as a whole, and can therefore lead to more effective teaching, both in the current year and in future years.

Whether assessments are carried out weekly, termly or annually, they still serve these two basic purposes, and they are essential if the process of continual improvement is to be effected. Ideally, such assessments reinforce the learning process, and well constructed tests have long been recognized as having this validity.

These are not the only two reasons for assessment, however, and it is the third and fourth that lead to more controversy and are more likely to be seen as wasting valuable teaching time.

The third reason for testing is to provide information for potential employers and higher education institutions. I would not seriously suggest that this is an unreasonable expectation: the unreasonable expectations arise when the institutions cannot agree on the information they want or when the information they want is so time-consuming to produce that it seriously affects the learning process for students. The latter is the key worry about SATs, where initial efforts at fulfilling the legal requirements of the National Curriculum led to teachers in trial schools being equipped with long checklists of skills and knowledge that were supposed to be checked for in every individual in the class at the same time as the class was being taught.

The fourth purpose of testing is to try to judge how well particular schools are doing in comparison with others. Again, this book is not the place to discuss the issue in detail, but schools cannot ignore the power of examination results as a 'Performance Indicator' – nor have they really been able to in the past.

The reason for highlighting these simple but important principles first is that if they can be kept in mind when the more mundane task is being undertaken in schools of translating the theory of testing and assessment into practice, then a sense of proportion and perspective can (I hope) be maintained. The rest of this chapter, dealing as it does with baseline assessments, the organization of internal and external examinations, and further means of assessment (including Records of Achievement) is intended to reflect this sense of proportion.

BASELINE ASSESSMENTS

Baseline assessments are designed to establish the prior attainment and potential of individual children. This information can then be used to ensure that they achieve as best they can. For teachers of pupils above Key Stage 1 (ie from Year 3 onwards) SATs may be used for this purpose. Increasingly, schools are also adding their own form of standardized assessment at the end of each year, so that progress between, say, Year 3 and Year 4 can be monitored. If this serves to improve the achievement of individual children, it can be viewed as beneficial to all concerned.

However, it has to be recognized that SATs (which are increasingly being used as a baseline assessment) were established to monitor and test schools, not children. The publication of SATs results, together with the league tables produced from GCSE and 'A' level examinations, can have unintended effects: for example, some secondary schools have concentrated on those students who could gain five A–C grades, to the detriment of others, while it would not be unnatural for primary schools to concentrate on getting a certain number of students up to level 4.

At the time of writing, we are also in the interesting position that external Key Stage 3 SATs only exist for English, Maths and Science. Teachers of non-core subjects are somewhat on the horns of a dilemma: do they feel relieved that these tests do not apply to their subject, or do they feel concerned at the risk of their subject therefore being downgraded in the eyes of parents and students? From the point of view of a deputy head with responsibility for assessment and examinations, it is important to be aware of the issues and to recognize that the lack of enthusiasm of staff for reasonable assessment may be due to factors (such as resentment about league tables and SATs) that are not of the school's making.

In a secondary school it will also be necessary to decide how CATs (or similar tests) will be administered, particularly by whom. Options include it being done through the English, Maths and Science departments, through tutors, or as a year group.

SCHOOLS INTERNAL EXAMINATIONS

Many secondary schools set aside a week or longer for internal examinations. It used to be the case that this happened at the end of a term and often involved the whole school taking examinations at one time. For various reasons (not least the convenience and sanity of the teachers) it is now more usual for such examinations to take place at different times of the year for different year groups, thus spreading the load of marking and also linking them more closely to such things as Year 10 option choices, entry for external examinations, school reports and parents' evenings.

Table 6.1 sets out a starting point for a possible timetable for internal examinations, and such a timetable – once constructed for your school – could be presented through the usual consultative structure that exists. The notes to the table indicate the reasons why the particular timings have been suggested.

It is important to get agreement on internal examination timings during a summer term for the following academic year and to ensure that

Table 6.1 *Internal examinations timings*

DATE	GROUP	ACTION
Nov/Dec	Year 11	Alert possible GCSE underperformance in time to take remedial action.
January	Sixth Form	As trials for GCSE and 'A' levels.
February	Year 9	In preparation for Year 10 option choices.
April	Year 8	To boost work and to allow for fact that their next ones will be in February in Year 9.
May/June	Year 10	To boost work and to allow for fact that their next ones will be in November/ December.
June/July	Year 7	To give idea of progress in first year.
July	Sixth Form	For Lower Sixth 'A' level students.

the agreed dates are entered on the annual school calendar. It is usual also to mark the date of external examination periods on any such calendar. Make sure that the school office knows all relevant dates, since most parents actually try to avoid taking their children on holiday during school examination periods, in contrast to the occasional ones who will even take them on holiday during SATs or GCSE examinations. (I was actually asked by one parent many years ago to rearrange a GCSE examination for her daughter, and when I explained bemusedly that this could not be done I was not totally surprised when her mother withdrew her from the examination!)

Once the dates have been entered in the school calendar, it will be your responsibility to make sure that suitable arrangements are made well in advance for the examinations to take place. You will need to work out your own personal timetable for this, since you must remind others of the dates and not vice versa. The arrangements will include deciding the venue (hall or classrooms?), sorting out suitable stationery (provided centrally or by departments?), setting out the actual examinations timetable, arranging invigilation (by own teachers or by others? – and do not forget breaks) and ensuring notification to students.

The first thing you need to know is which departments want examinations, how many papers they want to set, how long each paper is to be and how many students are involved. This is usually more complicated for Year 11 and the sixth form than for Year 7, but even the arrangements for Year 7 require careful preparation. The first stage of this preparation is to circulate a form asking for the information you need, and Figure 6.1 gives an example you may find useful to adopt or adapt for your own use. Plan to have the information in response at least four school weeks before the actual examination period.

Some schools cancel all lessons for a year group during their examination period (more usual for Year 11 than for Year 7) and some even give 'study leave' (allowing older students to stay at home when they have not got examinations).

When you have gathered all the information, it is useful to look at the timetable and, assuming that students are not on study leave, try to block in examinations to cause as little disruption to other subjects as possible. This is particularly important when many subjects use continuous assessment and coursework, and may not actually require much in the way of formal examination time: they become quite understandably aggrieved if their attempts to maintain some lessons are made more difficult than they need be. In this matter, it is good management practice to ensure that general principles are discussed in the appropriate forum and agreement reached on them.

YEAR 10 INTERNAL EXAMINATIONS

The internal examinations for Year 10 students are scheduled to start on Wednesday 5 May 1999 and I should be grateful if you would complete and return this form to me by Friday 19 March 1999. Nil returns would be appreciated, but it will be assumed that any department not returning the form by 19 March will not require any formal examination provision.

You are reminded that departments have agreed to provide their own stationery and that examination papers for typing/copying should be left in the Office before the Easter break at the latest.

Thank you,
Jane Elliott

Department:

Subject(s):

Number of paper(s):

Length of paper(s):

Level:

Number of students:

Classes (or attach list):

Special requests/notes:

Figure 6.1 *Request for internal examinations*

Having pencilled in what looks like a timetable that meets the maximum of requests with the minimum of disruption, look at the implications for invigilation. If another deputy deals with 'cover', now is the time for the two of you to look together at the timetable since your colleague may have information about staff attending courses etc, which you will not. It is important that you agree exactly what each of you will do and make sure that staff also know these details.

After many years of providing invigilation timetables for all staff, colour coded for each week and carefully checked for mistakes, I have found that it is still necessary to provide some kind of reminder on the daily 'cover' list: this is the one place where most staff can be guaranteed to look, and those who do not look will be reminded of their invigilation duty by those who do. However, all staff should still have a copy, which should be legible – either typed or neatly written out in a clear hand. If you do not take the invigilation timetable seriously, why should anyone else?

Students should be given clear instructions on how to conduct themselves in a formal examination – and staff should also know what is permitted and what is not. Practices have changed over the years and also differ from one school to another; it is very important, therefore, that there is absolute consistency within the school. The simplest and best means of achieving consistency is to use the same procedures for formal internal examinations as for external ones, which has the value both of consistency and of encouraging sound practices. Try to ensure that new staff or supply teachers are not expected to invigilate on their own for the first few times. Remember also that when staff do invigilate on their own, there should always be a 'runner' available to get assistance if necessary – and this person needs to know to whom they should run!

EXTERNAL EXAMINATIONS

If the procedures for formal internal examinations have been modelled on the requirements of external examination boards (except possibly with regard to any restrictions on staff supervising in their own subjects), then external examinations should not cause a disproportionate amount of disruption to the life of the school.

The examination boards provide detailed instructions on how examination papers are to be stored, the number of invigilators required for different examinations, the space required between candidates, and so on. You need to read these carefully – and also note that boards do not all have exactly the same procedures. Try to read the instructions without preconceived ideas (some strange customs and practices that have been seen in schools have not in fact been rooted in actual requirements of examination boards at all) and try to read them carefully. For example, it makes a significant difference to the layout of an examination room if the centres of tables are required to be six feet apart, rather than the table edges; this may seem like a small point but it can make a substantial difference in real life.

Plan in advance what will happen if the fire alarm goes off or the heating breaks down (it can happen in a cold hall in this country in June). Make sure that the rest of the senior management team are aware of all the examination arrangements, partly to ensure that if you are absent there is proper provision made and partly to ensure that they realize how fine a job you are doing!

It might be worth mentioning a curious practice that I for one do not really understand but that does happen in at least some schools. When the Year 11 and 13 students have left school and are returning only for examinations, many staff are freed from teaching them. In most cases there are then more staff available for invigilation than are actually needed. This is an excellent opportunity for departments to organize the hundred-and-one things that any vibrant department would like to do. Even so, they sometimes find such 'catching up' impossible because so many of them have been used for invigilation. While it is important that staff do not sit in examination rooms marking books – they are there to invigilate – it is also important that they are allocated to this fairly monotonous activity in numbers that are seen to be sensible. In that way, you encourage proper invigilation procedures.

RECORDING ACHIEVEMENT

Formal examinations are only part of the assessment process and, indeed, most external examinations now include at least some element of course work. This section is headed 'Recording achievement' in the belief that all positive achievements should be noted somewhere in order to recognize achievement and to encourage more of it.

While government initiatives in the past have encouraged secondary schools to provide students with a formal Record of Achievement, many primary schools now have their own form of recording achievement and children very proudly carry these records with them when they move to secondary school. If you are responsible for primary–secondary transfer and/or assessment, it is important to know what the Year 7 students are used to already.

One obvious but sometimes neglected source of assessment data is students' exercise books and files. Every time a piece of work is ticked, some kind of assessment or judgement is assumed to have been made. Many secondary school departments have marking policies, and some schools have whole-school policies that work in practice (as opposed to theory), and that is certainly something to be encouraged. In addition, secondary school departments also operate various types of tests (for example, checking knowledge of vocabulary in modern languages) and assessments (for example, skills tests in science), particularly with the arrival of National Curriculum SATs. There is, therefore, likely to be a fair amount of recorded data available on each student's progress.

Standardization

A deputy head may have been given the responsibility of formalizing the recording of achievement and of getting some kind of standardization across the curriculum. There is a real dilemma here, in that the more standardization that occurs the less useful the outcomes of it are. Assessment should follow the curriculum, and therefore a varied curriculum is bound to lead to some variation in the resulting assessments. On the other hand, the review of a student's progress will be read by the student, the student's parents and possibly a potential employer, and therefore it needs to be intelligible and to look as if all the assessments have come from the same school.

If you are asked to assume responsibility for this standardization procedure, you should first of all ask to see what assessment is at present performed in departments and any plans that they have for developing new methods. In a primary school, you will need to look at the assessment practices of different teachers and/or different year groups. When you have studied these, you will be in a better position to try to summarize them. This exercise in itself will be educative, not just for you but for the rest of the staff, who may only have a vague idea of how different departments or teachers organize this seemingly common task.

You may wish at this stage either to produce a summary from the information you have in front of you or you may prefer to devise a suitable questionnaire to assist you in doing this. As the end product, you need to be able to have an overview of assessment and you need to share this with all staff.

It will become clear to staff that there is a variety of practice, but do not assume that this will automatically be seen as a bad thing. To get agreement on some moves towards standardization without doing serious damage to the variety and breadth of the curriculum, it will be necessary to pose some questions. These might include:

- ❏ For whom is the information intended?
- ❏ Will they understand it in its present form?
- ❏ How could it be made easier to understand?
- ❏ What student input is there?
- ❏ What is the role of the tutor or the individual teacher?

These questions will not only raise the issue of standardization but should also show the way forward in the area of student involvement in the process, leading to a useful Record of Achievement document at the end of a student's five, six or seven years at the school.

There are some things that may have to be decided on a majority vote – for example, whether an A–D, an A–E or a 1–6 grading is used for effort – but there are others where different departments can quite properly record assessments in a variety of ways. An example of this is where an English department has biannual skills assessments, while the PE department records details of performances in a wide range of sports' activities as they occur: both documents (the latter one, for instance, also recorded week by week on a computer) build up to provide a detailed record of achievement.

Using the tutor/adviser

Most secondary schools now recognize the importance of one member of staff acting as an adviser to students on an individual basis, and in most cases this is the tutor (or form teacher). In addition to proper training for this role, it is also necessary for detailed and adequate information to be provided to enable the tutor to have a meaningful discussion with each student assigned. The purpose of such a meeting is to enable a review of progress to take place and targets to be set for the future, and in the absence of detailed information this is very difficult. The input of the student is also essential if any change is to take place and the exercise is to have any purpose.

This is also a useful point at which to mention that it is not only academic achievement that should be acknowledged or recorded. Many of the ethical values and 'life' skills that are learned and displayed at school are of real benefit both there and then and in preparation for later life, and they may not show up in a record that is derived only from academic records. Try to construct a system that also takes such values and skills into account in its recording process.

Assistance in running the system

It is important to go back to first principles and to state clearly that assessment and the recording of it are a means to end, not an end in themselves. Therefore, every effort should be made to minimize the amount of time spent on it and to maximize the use of that freed time. There are many tools available – optical reading cards, computer programmes and the like – that can make the job more time-effective. They need to be used with caution, but they can contribute something to cutting down on the drudgery of recording assessments and thus leave more time for helping students to learn new things instead of spending too much time writing down yesterday's achievements. Yesterday's milestone is useful only in pointing the way towards tomorrow's.

Ancillary help has long been available to science and CDT departments. There is no logical reason why it should not be available to all departments to assist, *inter alia*, with recording achievement. Since the advent of LMS, and with the government's advice on minimizing administrative tasks for teachers, there is no real barrier to doing this on a reasonable scale.

POINTS TO NOTE

❏ Testing should come second to teaching.
❏ Establish the principles before the practice.
❏ Examinations should be planned well in advance.
❏ Invigilation should be kept in perspective.
❏ Accurate and readable information about students' attainment is needed.
❏ The tutor is the key to recording student achievement.
❏ The student must also be involved in the process.

7

FINANCE AND MANAGEMENT SYSTEMS

I did dream of money-bags tonight
(William Shakespeare)

Schools made a variety of organizational changes in response to LMS, some involving the employment of a bursar, sometimes with accountancy qualifications and sometimes without. In the majority of schools, the head teacher is responsible for the construction of the budget, which is then presented to the governing body for amendment and approval. In some cases a deputy head is given this responsibility, but even where this does not occur it is not unusual in some schools for a deputy head to be given the responsibility of monitoring the budget during the year and possibly of allocating 'capitation' allowances. Linked with this is often control of the management information systems, which are not exclusively for the management of finance but have been introduced in most schools in response to the specific need for detailed financial information.

This chapter will deal with three separate aspects of the task of controlling the finances of a school, some or all of which may be your responsibility:

1. the overall school budget;
2. 'capitation';
3. information systems.

It is assumed that LMS is well established in your school, but that many decisions on expenditure owe their existence to factors that existed before LMS (for instance, staffing and caretaking); setting up a new school with a new budget would allow for possibilities that are likely to take longer to find in the majority of schools. Long-term possibilities include changing the balance of the budget between staffing and other resources, generating substantial extra income, making local agreements on 'cover', and so on. All of these are increasingly being done in some schools at present, but they are not as yet universal practice. In the future, there is likely to be more variety in the ways in which schools manage their budgets. Your management task, as always, is to make sure that practice reflects intention.

For the purposes of this chapter, it will be assumed that the local education authority (LEA) will allocate money to the school. From April 1999 changes are being made to the exact ways in which this is to be done; however, this book does not deal with how or why money is allocated, since this is likely not to be of enormous practical help to deputy heads. From April 1999 or April 2000, schools will be able to take on the responsibility for more areas of expenditure and, at the time of writing, these areas were to include school meals, site maintenance, capital works, and so on. Grant-maintained schools have already held these responsibilities for some time. There is likely to be a great deal of variety in what happens in different areas – for example, in one LEA the schools may want control of repairs and maintenance expenditure, while in a neighbouring LEA they may not. This means that detailed knowledge of your school's delegation arrangements will be needed.

The examples given in this chapter deal with areas that are likely to be delegated to *all* schools. This is intended to make it easier for the new deputy head to see how a school budget is set, and additional items can be easily added when dealing with a real budget. A short glossary of terms used in this chapter is as follows:

❑ *Age-weighted-pupil-units (AWPUs)*: the amount of money given to each school based on the ages and numbers of pupils on the school roll.
❑ *Capital expenditure*: spending on such things as school buildings (but not routine maintenance).
❑ *Capitation*: cash allocated for the purchase of books, stationery, equipment, etc.
❑ *The formula*: usually refers to details of how LEAs propose to allocate the annual school budget.
❑ *On-costs*: the cost of the employers' contributions for national insurance and superannuation for employees.
❑ *Special Needs allocation*: the part of the school budget allocated to take account of such things as numbers entitled to free school meals.
❑ *Virement*: moving money from one heading (eg staffing) to another (eg capitation).

THE SCHOOL BUDGET

The LEA has the duty to inform the school of its annual budget before 1 April each year. The responsibility for the allocation of this school budget to different budgetary headings lies with the governing body of the school. Some choose to ask a working party to do the detailed work and make recommendations for the full governing body to accept or amend as they see fit; an advantage of this approach is that a smaller quorum is required for a full governing body to make such a decision than is required for a committee to do so.

Whatever approach is adopted, it is almost certain that if you are involved in budget preparation, you will be asked to provide detailed information and advice on the amounts to be allocated under different headings. More importantly, perhaps, is that you will need to be able to advise on whether the budget is adequate to pay for existing commitments (especially staffing) or whether steps will need to be taken to reduce these commitments (which could well mean declaring redundancies). It is not usual to plan for a budget deficit, although this can happen: if it does, the overspending will be taken from the following year's budget. Table 7.1 gives an example of recommendations that you might make to a governors' working party, given an LEA allocation of just over £1 million.

The headings chosen in our example for 'This School' are not the only ones that can be used: different LEAs tend to use slightly different headings

Table 7.1 *Budget share for This School, 1999–2000*

	£	£
Employee expenses		
Teachers' salaries	653 394	
Ancillary salaries	42 990	
Lunchtime supervision	5 630	
National Insurance	49 100	
Superannuation	56 060	
Other employee expenses	1 860	809 034
Running costs		
Furniture	1 590	
Laundry	170	
Capitation	38 280	
Swimming	3 000	43 040
Premises costs		
Water	1 100	
Sewerage and environmental	3 990	
General rates	59 160	
Energy	41 850	
Maintenance	7 350	113 450
Miscellaneous		
Caretaking and cleaning	64 460	
Grounds maintenance	11 250	75 710
Total budget share		1 041 234

in order to take account of differing local circumstances or accounting systems. A school also can modify the headings set by its LEA, but this should only be done gradually, since the LEA will be providing the governors with statements at the end of each financial year, and requiring forecasts of expenditure from your school, that are based on its own accounting system and not your school's. In practice, it is usually possible for schools to have budget headings that suit them, but it is important to note that there are often differences between those chosen and used internally and those used for outturn statements (statements of income and expenditure issued by LEAs to schools after the end of the financial year).

The figure for teachers' salaries is by far the largest item on the budget, particularly since most of the National Insurance and superannuation will be for teachers as well. 'Other employee expenses' will vary from one LEA to another (and for some will not appear on this form at all) but can include such things as staff travel and 'protected' allowances for redeployed staff from pre-LMS days.

'Capitation' refers to the part of the budget for books, stationery, materials, etc, and this used to be the only part of the budget that was under the control of the school. (There will be more detailed study of 'capitation' and its allocation later in the chapter.) Our example shows 'furniture' as a separate item, but in some cases this will be put together with capitation, or possibly with maintenance. 'Laundry' may cover an allowance paid to certain ancillary staff for laboratory coats, or it may relate to cleaning teachers' PE kit.

Rates and sewerage charges are likely to be fixed, while the figure for energy costs will have to be a guess – although it should be an informed one (which is no different from what we do in our own homes). Maintenance and internal decoration of the school would appear to be self-explanatory, but in fact there is a whole area of potential conflict between the school and the LEA over what each one should pay for (for example, if there is a flood in the school library because of a leaking roof, should the LEA pay to refurbish the library or should the school?).

In our example the costs of caretaking and cleaning are given as a separate sum; in some LEAs the staffing costs are put with 'employee expenses', while in others – certainly in the bigger schools – the contract for cleaning is separated from the costs of caretaking. Grounds maintenance is also dealt with in different ways in different LEAs.

The important thing for a deputy head dealing with the school budget is to be aware of local practice, while at the same time realizing that there are general management principles that need to be operated when setting out a proposed budget. These may be deduced by addressing the simple question, 'How do I go about suggesting the allocation of particular sums of money to particular items by the governors?' We shall look at this now, referring back to Table 7.1 for specific and detailed examples.

Allocating the school budget to various headings

Assuming that, for our example, the LEA has allocated £1,041,234 to the school for a 12-month period and that a deficit budget is not permitted, the total allocations must therefore add up to that amount. It is possible that the LEA will try to help the school predict what is needed under certain headings – some LEAs offer finance officers to help schools plan in advance – but in the end it is the school (in the shape of the governors) which must make the decisions. If the school has already operated a delegated budget, there will be historical figures to go on but, if not, then the burden of allocation is going to be so much greater. How can it be done?

Employee expenses

Setting a figure for employee expenses will necessitate having the following information:

❑ names of all employees to be paid by school;
❑ pay grades of employees – teachers, LEA scales, etc;
❑ the point on pay grades of each employee;
❑ any potential movements up pay scales (eg increments);
❑ award dates of annual pay increases;
❑ likely increases for different grades of employee;
❑ names of employees who are contracted-out for National Insurance purposes;
❑ names of employees who do not contribute to the LEA pension scheme;
❑ National Insurance rates;
❑ Pension contribution rates;
❑ names of staff who are only employed during term time;
❑ other factors.

Behind this seemingly straightforward list lies a lot of mystery. It may seem obvious that one needs the names of all the school's employees. However, early entrants to the game of delegated budgets will know that this is not necessarily a simple matter. Some examples that have emerged in different parts of the country of staff wrongly charged to school budgets include the following: staff paid under 'Section 11'; midday supervisors who no longer work in the school; the whole national insurance costs of teachers who are employed in LEA youth clubs instead of just the bit related to their teaching post; 'seconded teachers'; and teachers who are employed at more than one school (particularly supply teachers).

These are only occasional real-life examples, which in the days when the LEA paid the salaries did not matter: it made little difference whether the whole of the National Insurance costs were charged to a school – or indeed to the education budget – when the LEA was paying for it all anyway. Nowadays, however, it matters not only whether the school pays this, but also whether it is included in the education budget (as opposed to the youth and community budget) since there are fairly tight restrictions on how much the LEA can retain centrally and how much of the education budget has to be delegated. These limits on central funding and delegation will be even tighter after April 1999.

Pay grades are now very significant, and not only for financial reasons. Many teachers did not know how much their teaching colleagues earned, never mind their non-teaching colleagues. Now it is all part of the public budget, to be seen (at least in global terms) by governors and parents. More than one governor, with a background as an industrial/commercial manager, has asked why such a large proportion of the budget is spent on teachers' salaries.

Pay grades of non-teaching staff are also important nowadays, not only because of their immediate costs but also because of employment legislation (particularly on equal pay): if a similar school down the road pays a clerical assistant according to Scale 5 to do the same job as one of your school's clerical assistants who is on Scale 3, then your governors/LEA may find themselves before an industrial tribunal. The vast disparity between the pay of some teaching staff and some of the clerical staff in particular is likely to be more commonly known now that schools and governors are getting more and more information that they did not have previously. In addition, and possibly more significantly, governors with delegated budgets can now move staff up pay scales if they wish, within certain limitations. The latter point applies to teaching and non-teaching staff alike.

You will need to know which pay scales staff are on, which point they are at on the scale, and which staff will have increments due during the next financial year. There are fairly obvious incremental implications for most staff who are not already at the top of their scale, but you will also need to know which (if any) staff are likely to gain further qualifications that will entitle them to additional increments – in the case of a BEd this could mean up to £3000 pa extra. Part-time and supply teachers are also entitled to an annual increment, provided that they have worked for at least six months in aggregate during that time. You will need to know which (if any) teaching staff are on temporary allowances, whether there are seconded staff who are due to return during the year, whether there are any staff on temporary contracts, and whether the governors plan to move the head teacher or one or more of the deputies up the spinal point during the year.

National Insurance rates can be very complicated, since they are related to levels of earnings: thus an employee who moves from one rate of contribution to another may increase your bill by a larger-than-normal percentage. Equally, some employees may not be liable to pay National Insurance at all because of the lower earnings limit. Superannuation contributions are now optional for teachers, and some may choose not to belong to the occupational scheme: this is good news for the school, which will not then have to pay the employers' contribution. (Note, however, that you will fall foul of the law on at least two counts if you try to advise all your colleagues to withdraw from the scheme in order to help keep down costs!)

When one is used to working and being paid within the teachers' scales and conditions of service, it is easy to be unaware of the fact that there are different pay award dates for other employees. Nevertheless, you should certainly know that the normal award date for teachers is 1 April and that increments are normally awarded on 1 September, so that normal awards will apply in full in the budget for most staff, and an award given on 1 September will cost 7/12ths of the annual amount. If some staff are only employed during term-time (eg clerical assistants and midday supervisors), you will need to know what arrangements exist for payment during the school holidays.

Item 12 in the above list (other factors) is most interesting because it is a bit like 'Catch 22', in that you will only get the answers to questions if you know the questions; and you may not know the questions until you see the answers! Some questions you need to ask are:

❑ Do you still have staff on protected Social Priority Allowances and, if so, at what rate (£210 or £276 per annum)?
❑ Are staff entitled to London allowances?
❑ Are any staff on protected travel supplements because of a previous redeployment?
❑ Does the LEA pay a teacher on maternity leave or her replacement, and what happens if the school does not actually employ somebody to replace her during her leave?
❑ How much do your supply teachers cost? (You need to know their incremental point, since they are legally entitled to payment at their most recent highest incremental point for periods of a day or more.)
❑ Has the LEA made provision for union cover? If so, who on your staff is entitled to it? Will the LEA pay for replacement cover or for the cost of the teacher released for union duties, which can make a big difference?

Having answered these questions and done your computations, and having checked them thoroughly, you should have a fairly accurate figure to suggest for employee expenses. You are now ready to tackle the next part of the budget.

Running costs

Your best guide in allocating money under this heading is to look at historical figures and allow for price rises. If the school has spent £37,165 in the previous year on capitation items, an addition of 3 per cent for inflation will give you the figure of £38,280. In the long run the governors may wish to change this, but for the initial figure you are safest in using an objective formula such as the one suggested here (historical plus 3 per cent for inflation), and a similar approach can be used for the allocation for furniture. Laundry may be a guess, and swimming tuition is a figure that you may be able to agree with the LEA, assuming that the present curriculum is to continue to operate.

Premises-related expenses

Water rates, sewerage and environmental charges and general rates are likely to be fixed; your LEA should be able to give you an accurate idea of how much these are. Site maintenance and internal decoration are items where you should certainly seek LEA guidance, particularly with regard to historical spending. This may be more difficult to find than you imagine, since although the LEA will almost certainly have had a budget in the past for such items, they will not have spent exactly that amount on every school every year, probably preferring to spend a lot on schools A–E in one year, schools F–K in the next year, and so on. On account of their greater size, they will also have been able to allocate larger amounts of money if a school was suddenly the victim of a spate of vandalism or had problems with the fixative on floor coverings in several rooms in the one year.

Schools need to put in place a policy on routine maintenance and internal decoration. Again, it was easy enough, under an earlier regime, for an LEA (if it had the money) to paint a whole school every so many years, but an individual school may find this very difficult to plan.

Miscellaneous expenses

The school may find that it is part of an LEA contract for cleaning and grounds maintenance. If this is the case, then you may well be told how much you need to set aside for this. In the case of caretaking, the school may or may not be the employer, with all the implications of this. If the school is the employer, then the cost of salaries (including overtime and likely future pay awards) will need to be worked out in a similar way to that for teachers and other ancillary staff; the LEA will be able to provide pay scales and local pay agreements covering the placement of staff on them.

Increasingly, though, schools are contracting out whole budget items. Grounds maintenance and cleaning are commonly contracted out, although some schools prefer to employ their own cleaners or ground-staff. This is a trend that may well continue, given that many businesses outside education now prefer to contract out 'non-core' functions.

Hidden expenses

The use of broad categories in the budget set out in Table 7.1 can hide a number of expenses that may catch you unawares. For example:

❏ Which heading covers the cost of the school brochure?
❏ Who pays for the school's television licence?
❏ Where does the money for refuse collection come from?
❏ Are the school cookers rented?
❏ What insurance cover is provided by the LEA and what does the school need to buy?
❏ Is it possible to have a reserve fund for emergencies?
❏ How much is the LEA going to charge for clerking governors' meetings?

As government pressure on LEAs to devolve more and more of the General School Budget to schools has increased, so there have been more items that schools have to pay for. It is likely, therefore, that this list of hidden expenses will increase rather than decrease, particularly after April 1999.

The broad view

In order to be specific, much of this chapter has dealt with one way of setting out the budget. However, it should be reiterated that there are different ways of setting out the information and you need to become familiar with your own LEA's approach. Whatever that approach is, there needs to be a general management strategy comprising several stages.

The first stage is to cost all expenditure items under the appropriate headings, as has been done above. The next stage is to look at the amount allocated by the LEA and see whether it equals the total of the estimates of expenditure (a miracle, for which you must hasten to claim the credit!), it is less than is needed by your school (a scenario with which some schools are all too familiar), or it is more than needed.

Spending a surplus

If there is more than is needed, then the governors can consider – at their leisure – how this should be spent. In this case, they have various options open to them, including:

❏ employing extra teachers, either permanently or for a specific purpose over a fixed term (eg to allow for staff training in the use of technology);
❏ employing additional ancillary staff;
❏ buying extra equipment, such as new technology, or replacing equipment that is near the end of its useful life;
❏ refurbishing and/or developing all or part of the school;
❏ providing funds for students to go on extra-curricular trips;
❏ increasing the funding for staff development;
❏ employing a foreign-languages assistant; or even
❏ putting aside money for contingencies and/or future planned expenditure.

It is important that the governors are made aware of whether this surplus is a one-off or likely to continue in the future, and whether there are likely to be changes in student numbers in the future that might affect their decisions. In the event of a surplus, there will be little pressure on the governors to make hasty decisions.

Dealing with a deficit

In the event of a deficit, the situation will be completely different from that where a surplus applies. If you have done your calculations of expenditure before receiving the LEA budget share, you will be able to see very quickly whether or not there is a deficit and, if so, how much it is. Let us suppose that the school budget share is to be £1,009,234, a deficit against expected requirements of £32,000. How can coping with this deficit be managed?

Your first task is to identify areas where savings can be made. It is not your responsibility actually to make these savings – even if you would like it to be; your job is to present facts and options to the governors (or to their appointed sub-committee or working party). So where can you suggest savings? Using the headings in Table 7.1's budget, the following comments are offered:

❑ *Teachers' salaries.* This is the largest item of expenditure and is the most likely area of saving: a 4 per cent reduction on this item in our example would nearly achieve the savings required. However, the curriculum might suffer with such a drastic reduction and redundancies might be required.

❑ *Ancillary workers' salaries.* Even a 10 per cent reduction on this item would save less than £5000 and could have a drastic effect on the support functions for staff. Most schools need more ancillary help, not less.

❑ *Lunchtime supervision.* It is unlikely that any savings can be made here, since many schools already operate with the minimum of supervisors required for safety.

❑ *National insurance.* This will be indirectly related to staff salaries (allowing for maximum and minimum earnings levels on which NI is paid), and so will reduce if staff salaries are reduced.

❑ *Superannuation.* Any change here will be directly related to salaries.

❑ *Other employee expenses.* There is little chance of saving much here in practice.

❑ *Furniture costs.* This could be cancelled but yields little in the way of savings; and it cannot be done for ever.

❑ *Laundry costs.* You are unlikely to make any significant savings in this area of expenditure.

❑ *Capitation.* Even allowing for items such as telephone costs, which will be reasonably fixed, one could probably save £10,000–£15,000 here if staff agreed to muddle through for a year with existing stocks of books and materials. But you need to consider the effect on the curriculum.

❑ *Swimming tuition.* No significant savings are feasible here unless a decision is taken to abandon or seriously reduce this provision.

❑ *Water charges.* A small saving may be possible here in the long term by the use of metering, but it is unlikely to be substantial or immediate.

❑ *Sewerage charges* These will be fixed costs.

❑ *Energy costs.* This particular item depends mainly on the weather and also partly on the cost of the different forms of energy consumed at the school. Energy costs can therefore be trimmed to some extent by a sensible energy-saving programme. Such a programme will take time to implement and may not yield much immediate saving, especially as few people would bet on a hot, dry winter or a gigantic cut in energy prices.

❑ *Maintenance costs.* This item already looks (in our example, at least) a very small sum of money to pay for a sudden rash of broken windows, never mind anything else. Some short-term savings might be possible, nevertheless.

❏ *Caretaking/cleaning*. You may have some control over this, in which case some savings might be made, but the full £32,000 savings needed in our example would require a 50 per cent cut in the this item's allocation.

❏ *Ground costs*. You may find it difficult to save on this in the short term, although some long-term savings may be possible.

The net result of looking for savings in this logical way is that there is little room for manoeuvre unless teaching staff reductions are considered.

Saving staff salary costs

In the past, making staff savings has been done – indirectly – in schools by the operation of redeployment schemes; however, nowadays under LMS there are significant differences of approach.

First, staff declared surplus may become redundant, since LEAs cannot force other schools to accept them as they could under redeployment; in any case, schools with money to spare may choose to spend it on equipment rather than on staffing. Secondly, under the previous system, schools would negotiate on the basis of the curriculum with their education officers, who could agree to protect them from the full impact of staff reductions. Thirdly, reductions were declared as a specific number of teachers, whereas now it is related to actual money. Given that individual members of staff cost different amounts of money – a Group 4 deputy can cost twice a standard-scale teacher – this can put pressure on governors to make older, more expensive staff redundant. Lastly, decisions on redeployment were ultimately made by the LEA; although they usually took curriculum advice from the head teacher and his or her senior management team. Now any redundancies must be declared within the school, and the finger of accusation is pointed very clearly at the senior management team who has provided the advice on which the governors act.

This is not the place to deal with the significance of employment legislation for the governors of the school, but it is important to note that when you present your options for savings in the budget to the governors the latter are clear about the timescale and procedures involved. First, it is the governors who declare the number of likely redundancies, and they should be working to clearly stated criteria for declaring the individual(s) to be affected. Any member of the senior management team who gives an opinion on who is likely to be nominated for redundancy risks the possibility of an appeal against that redundancy being successful.

Secondly, time is relevant to the process in two ways. It is usually recommended by LEAs that four weeks' notice is given for discussion with the unions and then two weeks for the individuals to be named and notified. If this is not done by 31 May, with the redundancy effective from 1 September, then the next effective date will be 1 January. Given that the Easter break usually takes up two weeks of the period April/May and that 31 May often falls in the spring half-term holiday, it can effectively mean that the number of redundancies at your school needs to be declared within a week or two of receiving notification of the school's budget share (which may not be until the end of March). The second way in which time is highly relevant is that the school budget operates from April to March but redundancies will be effective from 1 September. This means that teaching staff declared redundant will still have to be paid for 5/12ths of the financial year. Thus, in order to save £32,000 in the financial year in our example, we would be looking not at one-and-a-bit teachers being displaced but nearer three.

The most difficult part of the process is that very few people want to make staff redundant. However, if it has to be done, then it is important that it is done professionally and on the basis of carefully prepared curriculum and financial planning.

Many schools have found that they can make some savings during the year, particularly by virement (ie reapportionment) from one budget head to another. A mild winter might just let this happen, where underspending on energy costs might be allocated elsewhere. It is also possible to allocate the money one would normally leave for supply cover to save on redundancy: this would require full staff consultation, however, since there are times during the year when a school does not need supply cover for sickness and times when more than one such supply teacher is needed. Some schools have managed to minimize redundancies among their caretakers by agreeing to vire some of the maintenance money in return for the caretakers doing some work in the school.

Sparks of hope

It is possible, of course, to balance your school's budget not by reducing expenditure but by increasing the income of the school. However, this is more likely to bear fruit in the long-term rather than the immediate financial year; it certainly is unlikely to save having to declare redundancies. Donations from the business world – possibly of materials rather than money – can help a school in this way. Unfortunately, however, the experience of many schools is that only a few can make any substantial gains from the business world, and in some cases they can only do so by spending a disproportionate amount of staff's skills on things other than that for which they have been trained.

In the final analysis, the allocation of money is supposed to reflect the aims and purposes of the school. It is the responsibility of senior management in particular to ensure that the management structures of the school serve this end. An open management style does seem to bring some benefits, even where staff do have to be declared redundant – at least the thinking behind the decisions can be clear to all. Whatever happens over budget deficits, there are still students to be educated, whose future depends on the effective management of the school. Staff morale is crucial to its success and needs to be maintained even – no, especially – in times of financial pressure.

CAPITATION

Whereas not long ago head teachers made the decisions on how much departments should get for books, materials and stationery, nowadays the management of what is known in schools as 'capitation' has evolved to a stage where many schools consult staff representatives on how it should be spent. In many cases this responsibility is delegated to a deputy head teacher. This section of the chapter looks at how you can exercise the responsibility of managing the capitation allowance in co-operation with staff, so that its effectiveness in helping the learning process can be maximized.

For the purposes of illustration, it will be assumed that the amount allocated in the budget in Table 7.1 (£38,280) is the amount to be spent. The management of this process can be used to enhance the delegation of responsibility to middle management and hence the effective management of the school: when middle managers feel involved in the process, they are more likely to try to make it work. One way of doing this is suggested here: each school will have to make its own decisions and devise its own structures, but this framework should serve as an example for modification or adaptation as necessary.

The finance committee

A representative committee of staff may be constituted in several ways. It needs to be large enough to encompass a range of views but small enough to be able to make specific recommendations to the head teacher on how the money should be spent. A group of six or seven staff, plus the deputy head responsible, offers a reasonable compromise; it may be that the head and one or more of the other deputies will sit in on the deliberations.

However, if a vote is necessary, I feel that only elected staff representatives should vote. The head or senior management team has in any case the power to veto any of the recommendations; and another potential difficulty is that if the members of the senior management team have voting rights they could exercise a 'block' vote which would be unhelpful to the consultation process.

If it is decided that there will be seven staff representatives, then the staff should be divided into seven roughly equal groups for voting purposes. In the case of a large department, such as English, Maths or Science, you may find that you have a natural constituency, but other departments may need to be grouped together. It is my view that it does not really matter whether the subjects concerned have a natural 'affinity' together (eg the humanities) or not (eg PE and modern languages), provided that it is clear that the elected members of the committee are responsible for representing the views of their constituents at committee meetings and for reporting back the decisions taken. Some schools may feel that representation through subject areas will give a broad enough perspective, while others may feel that there should be a separate 'pastoral' representative; this is a decision to be taken in each school in its own circumstances.

In my experience, heads of large departments are usually in favour of being members of the finance committee, provided that it is seen to be a meaningful forum. Some heads and deputies throw up their hands in horror at the implicit democracy of such a committee. The power of veto exists, but if it is regularly used the committee will cease to be seen as important and heads of department will condemn it as a sham. Therefore, it is generally the case that recommendations made by the committee are de facto decisions.

The questions most frequently asked about such a structure are, 'But don't they all want to spend money on their own departments?' 'Who looks after the interests of small departments?', 'How do you get agreement to spend on whole-school items?' and 'How does the head get his/her own way under such a system?' The answer to the last question is that the head gets his/her own way by having persuasive arguments. The answers to the other questions depend on how the committee operates, which is largely down to you. Essentially, the spending of money does not happen in a vacuum, and how it is done reflects the management ethos and style of the school. I would suggest that the following points are essential if the process is indeed not to become a source of contention and division:

❏ *Openness.* All information provided for members of the committee should be displayed at the same time on the staff room noticeboard.

❏ *Accountability.* Every member of the committee has a 'constituency' of staff. Thus every member of staff has direct access to a member of the committee, who is responsible for explaining the rationale of all decisions reached.

❏ *Ethos.* Every opportunity should be taken to emphasize the corporate nature of the school, not just in matters of finance but in all matters. Sectionalism needs to be discouraged on all fronts at all times, so that staff feel that their interests are served by the school and vice versa.

❏ *Peer pressure.* Any requests for extra money or special consideration should be on the basis either of agreed criteria (for instance a sudden increase in the number of GCSE students), which can then be operated by the deputy head, or of published requests. If the ethos referred to above exists in the school, this will act as a regulatory brake on individual departments or faculties persistently asking for extra money.

❏ *An agreed formula.* This refers to a rationale, agreed by the committee, for how money is allocated.

❏ *The atmosphere of each meeting.* Earlier we referred to voting rights, an issue that ought to some degree to be hypothetical. You should start each meeting with the intention of reaching agreement on proposals. If there are regular votes, particularly with narrow majorities, there is something wrong.

❏ *Strategy.* Staff need to feel that a long-term view is being taken of finance, and that even if a department fails to get money for proposed developments in a particular year they have a good chance of getting it in the next year. This encourages hope and also encourages middle management to take a longer-term view of the development of their area of responsibility.

❏ *Governors' involvement.* When the committee has been running for a while and feels confident in its operation, it may be a good idea to invite one or two governors to attend meetings. The presence of governors, particularly parent–governors, can help reinforce the corporate ethos of the school.

❏ *Respect.* In any meeting, all views should be considered on their merit and not on who happens to be putting them forward.

A key point that needs to be reiterated time and time again is that good management creates good schools. Staff will give far more commitment and energy to a cause that they believe in, and to an institution where they have real involvement. People only hide behind the barricades of their own departments when they do not feel confident about stepping out on to the open courtyard that ought to be the school. Effective middle managers, with their own groupings, are needed for a large institution like a school to be effective, but they are a means to an end not an end in themselves.

One could summarize the management of capitation by saying that it is mostly about the management of people and hardly at all about 'pounds and pence'. However, it can be useful to look at the pounds and pence to see how the philosophy argued here can operate in practice.

Pounds and pence

Let us suppose that the sum of £38,280, indicated in Table 7.1, has been allocated for capitation and that you have just taken over responsibility for the finance committee. Let us also assume that a committee structure similar to that outlined above already exists and that there are agreed general criteria (including 'weightings') for allocating money.

The money available can be divided into three parts:

1. centrally funded items;
2. running costs for subjects;
3. 'bid' money.

Figure 7.1 suggests the agenda for the first meeting of a (fictitious) finance committee in the financial year 1999–2000, with notes of explanation attached. Comments are offered on some of the items included in the capitation list in Figure 7.1.

Centrally funded items

The cost of telephones is a constant source of friction in many schools. It needs to be kept in perspective and the finance committee can help with this. If savings on telephone costs can be seen quite clearly as being fed back into the money for books, materials and equipment, then the help of the finance committee can be sought in trying to keep them under control.

My own experience some years ago was very illuminating. For the nth time the telephone bills in the school had increased by more than the cost of inflation. We decided to put the problem to the finance committee, and the issue was thoroughly debated there. It was decided that only certain telephones would be programmed to make other than local calls, that all telephones would have a sticker attached saying 'Calls cost money; fewer calls mean more books', that another sticker would illustrate the difference

SCHOOL CAPITATION BUDGET, 1999–2000

There will be a meeting of the finance committee on Monday 26 April 1999 at 3.45 pm in the Conference Room.

Agenda

1. Minutes of previous meeting.
2. Consideration of budget for 1999–2000
3. Any other business.

Notes

The governors have allocated £38,280 for capitation this year. I estimate that 'centrally funded' items will cost as follows:

	£
Telephones	3 000
Postage	900
Photocopier lease	2 100
Minibus	300
Administration	1 600
Duke of Edinburgh scheme	300
Camps	300
French exchange visit	150
Resources	1 000
Library	1 000
Information technology	400
Staff travel	700
Miscellaneous	500
School brochure	1 500
Reserve	2 000
Total	15 750

This will leave a balance of £22,530 for allocation to 'running costs' and 'bids'. We need to decide (a) how much to allocate to each item and (b) dates for submission of 'bids'.

If you have any queries or wish to add items to the agenda, please see me before the meeting.

Thank you,
Jane Elliott
March 1999

Figure 7.1 *Finance committee agenda*

in cost between calls before and after 1 pm (such a differentiation still existed at the time) and that every telephone would have a sheet beside it for staff to record private calls. The important point about this illustration is that it was not the head teacher who made these decisions but the finance committee. They could see that savings would feed directly back into the classrooms in the form of more resources. The feeling of 'them' and 'us', which this issue often engenders in schools, was avoided. There were two positive outcomes: the relative cost of the telephones went down; and the issue was removed as a source of constant friction every three months.

Looking at Figure 7.1 again, we can see that the photocopier leasing cost in our example is funded centrally but copy costs are not. An important factor here is that the first can be forecast accurately while the other cannot. You may find including the leasing cost in the cost charged to departments for copies means having to forecast how many copies would be done during the year (so as to add the correct amount to each copy). Unfortunately this can prove very difficult to do, and so 'This School' has decided to fund the leasing centrally, leaving departments to pay for direct copy costs and paper alone.

The amounts under the headings of 'resources', 'information technology', 'library', 'Duke of Edinburgh scheme', 'camps', 'minibus' and 'the French exchange' are only hypothetical examples of decisions that schools might make to fund these items, which are not related to student numbers. Although fictitious figures, they do give some indication of where the school places its priorities.

The item 'miscellaneous' is there to provide for unexpected items, and 'reserve' is to allow for overspending or very large unexpected items. In theory this 'reserve' ought to be self-financing after the first year, particularly if overspending and underspending by departments is carried forward (a very good way of training middle managers in the effective use of resources).

When the finance committee meets, it is likely that some time may be spent going through these central items and making comments. It may even be the case that some of them will be changed, but normally decisions to stop funding, for example, 'camps' should initially be taken through the normal curriculum consultative channels.

Running costs for subjects

Once the centrally funded items have been discussed and agreed, the school's finance committee has to decide how to divide the balance of £22,530 between 'running costs' and the 'bid' system.

'Running costs' refers to the amount of money that is given to departments each year to provide stationery, expendable materials (eg chemicals, wood and fabrics) and the replacement of some books that may have been lost or become unusable. The figure is related to student numbers taught and for how many periods, with weightings for age of students and for the nature of the subject. Points for each subject are allocated on this basis and added up, and the point score is then used to divide up whatever money is allocated to running costs proportionately across subjects. A simple example will help to make this clear.

Let us suppose that there are 500 students on the roll (in an 11–16 school), 200 being in Years 10–11 and 300 in Years 7–9, and that all students study English and Science. The agreed 'weightings' are 1 for students in Years 7–9, and 1.5 for students in Years 10 and 11. There are also subject 'weightings' of 1 for English and 2 for Science. The points scores for these subjects can be calculated as in Table 7.2.

These numbers are only illustrative but show how the calculations are worked out. A few comments should be added here. First, the pupil numbers are very convenient in this example; in real life they will not be. A decision will need to be taken on how many students will be starting in Year 7 (or whatever your school's intake year happens to be); on balance, departments will not gain or lose very much if you get the figure a bit wrong. Secondly, implicit in the calculation basis given above is that the finance committee has reached agreement in the past on subject and age weightings: do not expect either an easy or a final decision on subject weightings until someone somewhere comes up with an objective valuation of the relative costs of teaching different subjects.

Table 7.2 *Point score calculations for running costs*

SUBJECT	YEAR	STUDENTS	PERIODS	AGE FACTOR	SUBJECT FACTOR	POINTS
English	7	100 ×	5 ×	1 ×	1	= 500
	8	100 ×	4 ×	1 ×	1	= 400
	9	100 ×	4 ×	1 ×	1	= 400
	10	100 ×	4 ×	1.5 ×	1	= 600
	11	100 ×	3 ×	1.5 ×	1	= 450
					Total points:	= 2 350
Science	7	100 ×	3 ×	1 ×	2	= 600
	8	100 ×	3 ×	1 ×	2	= 600
	9	100 ×	3 ×	1 ×	2	= 600
	10	100 ×	5 ×	1.5 ×	2	= 1 500
	11	100 ×	5 ×	1.5 ×	2	= 1 500
					Total points:	= 4 800

Let us now return to the decision to be taken on how to divide the cash between 'running costs' and 'bids'. Let us suppose, for the sake of simplicity, that the decision reached is to leave a round figure of £10,000 for 'bids'. This means that there will be £12,530 for running costs. The way in which you calculate how much each department will get is to add the total points scores for all departments and to divide this into the available £12,530. This will give a monetary value to each 'point' and therefore, each department will get, for running costs, their total points score multiplied by this unit monetary value. For example, if the total points for all departments add up to 20,000, then £12,530 ÷ 20 000 will give a monetary value of £0.6265 to each point. In our example, English has 2350 points and will therefore get an allocation of £1472.28, and Science has 4800 points and will get an allocation of £3007.20.

It should be noted that moving to a system that leaves money for bids will reduce what some subjects have got in total in previous years. You may need to make two points to your colleagues about this. First, departments will be able to bid for a share of the £10,000 set aside. Secondly, previous allocation systems may not have been fair: there certainly used to be a feeling in many schools (whether justified or not) that the head allocated capitation money on a whim.

The point about the procedure outlined here is that it is based on management principles and that published criteria will be used. It is important that this is understood, particularly by members of the finance committee whose task it will be to explain it to their 'constituents'. It may be advisable in the first year of any such scheme to allow for 'transitional relief' where departments suffer a drastic reduction in their normal funding. It does need to be said here (although perhaps not loudly in the staff room!) that some departments in some schools have been more generously funded than others with comparable numbers of students and resource needs, and the effect of this may have been to lead to wastefulness.

The positive side of all this is that when you devolve real financial responsibility to departments, they become more efficient in using and conserving resources. I favour charging departments for stationery and for photocopying; if you do not, you have to set aside a large amount of money to pay for these, and you remove any incentive to departments to economize. Effective management is all about delegating responsibility, and the real financial power that is needed to go with it.

The bid system

In our example we have assumed that £10,000 has been set aside for 'bids'. Once an amount has been thus set aside, departments are invited to request extra money for specific projects. Any requests for extra money for whole-school items – for example, a new audio-visual system or more televisions – should also be submitted at this time. A suggested form for these purposes is shown in Figure 7.2.

Departments should be encouraged to limit their reasons for their proposal to the space provided. The question on spreading the bid over more than one year is to allow for a curricular development (eg the new GCSE course for French) to be funded when needed; there will need to be a commitment now about future funding in 2000–2001. A major innovation, such as SMP maths, will need to have a commitment for at least five years ahead.

The departmental contribution would be relevant where a new course is being purchased, since part of the allocation of running costs that departments get is meant to replace some books each year. It needs to be made clear that the 'bid' system is meant to provide for one-off items (even if such an item is spread over more than one year), and it is not intended that departments will abuse it by applying for extra money every year.

When you have received all the bids, you should summarize items and amounts on one sheet, photocopy this together with supporting documentation, and circulate the pack to committee members (including a copy on the staff room notice board). The next finance committee meeting then has to decide on the merits of each one and allocate the £10,000 accordingly. Partial funding (especially of something like a new GCSE course) is not usually a good idea, so the decision on each bid can be to grant it, to defer it with a promise of reconsidering it next year, or to reject it.

The decisions taken on each item should be minuted and circulated. If a bid has been deferred or refused, then you should see the person who submitted it and explain the reasons for the decision; it is perfectly proper to bind the committee to secrecy until you have done this. Some committees invite anyone making a bid to attend the meeting, present their arguments and answer questions. The atmosphere in which the meeting is conducted is critical and is your responsibility as chairperson. It is usually a good idea to remind members of the committee that all bids need to be considered on merit and prioritized, and it will only be lack of resources that means having to maybe defer those of recognized merit.

Finally, it should be mentioned that some departments find it easier than others to attract extra funds from outside the school – for example, some benefactors will find it attractive to partly fund the provision of a new technology room, or a local firm may provide some materials for the

BID FOR EXTRA FINANCE FOR YEAR 1999–2000

Department: Amount:

Item(s):_____

Reasons in support of bid:

_____
_____
_____
_____
_____
_____
_____
_____
_____
_____
_____
_____
_____
_____
_____
_____
_____
_____
_____

Can this bid be spread over more than one year?

How much is the department contribution?

Please return this form to Jane Elliott by Friday 21 May 1999

Figure 7.2 *'Bid' sheet for extra finance*

science department. Information about such extra funds should be publicly available since such information may have a bearing on whether a
particular bid will be granted. The point is that any resources given belong
to the school and the school belongs to the students – and the finance
committee is part of the management structure that is supposed to be
maximizing the effectiveness of the whole curriculum received by the students, not just little bits of it.

MANAGEMENT INFORMATION SYSTEMS

The school will be held accountable to the LEA for how it spends not only
the money allocated by the LEA itself but also money from others. The
LEA is responsible for providing the school with the tools it needs to dis-
charge its accountability. These tools will include staff training and development, as well as adequate information about items of expenditure.
Aspects of the former are considered in Chapter 8, while aspects of the latter are discussed below.

Finance information systems

There are two kinds of computerized information systems that are likely
to be available to schools to assist with their financial responsibilities
under LMS. The first kind are stand-alone (or networked) personal computers, which the school can use to prepare forecasts and to check their
expenditure. The other is the mainframe computer based at County Hall
(or its equivalent). In some LEAs these are connected, but in many they
still are not. Assuming that they are, you will be using the mainframe to
find what has been charged to your school, and your school computer(s)
to keep a running check on your spending. In some LEAs, schools do not
have direct access to the mainframe computer and the information on
expenditure is given to the school in the form of computer printouts or
floppy disks.

It is essential that training is available not only to the deputy head
responsible for finance but also to the office staff who will be assisting
with the day-to-day running of the budget. Other members of the senior
management team will need some knowledge of the system(s), and heads
of department may need some in-house training on the printouts they
will be receiving. There is no doubt that some of the systems that are now
in schools are already allowing them to keep a much tighter control of
capitation spending than used to be the case; heads of department are

likely to welcome some of the detailed printouts of their spending – provided that they can understand them!

The list below gives a series of tips/suggestions intended to maintain your sanity and help you actually begin to manage (rather than passively cope with) the school's budget:

❏ Do not accept the blame either for failing to do the impossible or for things that are not your fault.

❏ Concentrate on getting information from the LEA mainframe computer and checking it: this is what you will be charged, not what your school computer says.

❏ Spend more time looking for errors in large items (such as staff salaries) than small ones (such as income from the sale of student coursework).

❏ Remember that LEA officers are doing their best and can sometimes provide very pertinent advice.

❏ Do not spend hours feeding the data to the computer that is automatically supposed to update staff salaries for you until you know that it actually does do so and that it will take less time to feed in the data than working it out with a ready reckoner and a calculator.

❏ Make sure that you get properly trained clerical help to manage the day-to-day running of the budget, and then that they are properly paid so that you do not lose them.

❏ Document all known errors (such as staff wrongly charged to your school) and notify the LEA: if they fail to correct it promptly it is not your fault or your problem.

❏ Much – maybe even most – relevant information about budget changes does not come via official channels but in off-the-cuff remarks from politicians or LEA officers.

❏ DO NOT PANIC – it solves nothing.

The suggestions are based on the principle that a school is obligated to do its best to manage LMS, whereas if the software is full of bugs, if the LEA cannot provide the information needed, or if the governors make a mess of their redundancy procedures, it is not your fault. At the end of the day, the LEA can take back a budget if the school does not operate it properly, but if the LEA itself is the cause of this failure, it will find it doubly difficult to operate it.

Other information systems

Linked in with the provision of finance information systems is often the provision of a package (usually within the same computer and in some way linked to the finance package) that allows for recording student details and numbers, planning and/or printing a timetable, recording students' achievements, and so on. You may find yourself in charge of this system, although most of the actual working on it will be done by the office staff. It is not possible to give detailed advice on a range of different proprietary systems, but it is worth making three general management points.

1. Any such system is a means to an end. For example, lists of students can be produced in different formats (as the software permits) without the need for typing them out each time. It can be helpful, say when organizing a school trip, to have a list of students in a certain year who stay for school dinners. You do need to remember, however, that the office staff will need training to use the system and also it may take a long time to put all the information into the computer system in the first place. A planned, realistic programme needs to be drawn up for this initial input.
2. These systems have changed the conditions of work for our clerical staff in many ways. This situation needs to be handled carefully but positively, so that the office staff do not, for example, have to stop answering the telephone when the printer is operating.
3. The need to plan work is heightened by such systems. Teachers sometimes assume that a list can be produced at the touch of a button on the computer. This is generally true – but only up to a point! The computer system will not produce a list if the school secretary is answering the telephone or is in the middle of using the computer to access the LEA's mainframe computer, if the computer has developed a fault, or if the software does not provide for exactly the list a teacher wants.

Evaluation of systems

Now that schools are in the position of spending their own money, they need to evaluate such systems. As part of that evaluation process, it should be your policy to ensure that your chosen system is providing the information the school wants as efficiently and cheaply as possible. That is what business people do in order to establish cost-effectiveness in their firm, and it is a way of working with which providers of hardware and software ought to be familiar.

POINTS TO NOTE

❏ Money is a means to an end, not the end in itself.
❏ Staffing issues need to be handled professionally.

❑ LMS assumes local decision making.
❑ Staff should be trusted to spend capitation sums.
❑ Accountability can be likened to responsibility.
❑ A school's spending indicates its real priorities.
❑ Management information systems are a means to an end.

8

STAFF DEVELOPMENT

When work is more exciting, people want to do it longer
(RM Kanter)

When we looked at the school budget we saw that normally well over 80 per cent of it was spent on staff salaries. Given this fact, is it not strange that little if anything is spent on staff training and development?

Until relatively recently it was possible for a classroom teacher to go through 40 years of teaching with virtually no training apart from initial teacher training – and even this was not obligatory 30 years ago! Such a teacher started teaching in the 1960s, and quite a few things have changed since then in our knowledge of the nature of learning, in the resources available for learning, in the environment in which young people live, and so on. Changes in education – including fundamental ones such as comprehensive education for all to the age of 16 and mixed-ability (now 'all-ability') teaching – were often introduced without any preparation of those teachers expected to carry them through in the schools. Exhortation and political belief were felt to be preparation enough. How strange!

There has been some improvement in recent years, and most staff now find at least some training offered to them that they can't avoid, if only on INSET (In-Service Education and Training of Teachers) days. The term 'avoid' is used advisedly because it is a sad fact that the quality of a lot of INSET is so poor that staff have to be forced to sit through it. To change the general climate in education towards a positive belief in the value – and, indeed, the necessity – of continual training and updating of skills will take time. Some schools are moving in this direction with great speed, but even they express dissatisfaction with their rate of progress.

In this chapter we shall look at ways in which the deputy head responsible for staff development can begin to chart ways forward in this crucial area of school management. Tom Peters provides a memorable phrase in his book, *Thriving on Chaos* (Harper and Row, 1987), in which he addresses the chronic lack of training in industry: 'A national disgrace, an epic opportunity.' How can we take this opportunity? We shall explore the possibilities in this chapter.

A BELIEF IN PEOPLE

There must first of all be a belief in people and in their ability to grow into their jobs. This principle needs to be enshrined very clearly in the School Development Plan and needs to embrace all staff, not just teachers. (Although your main task will be the development of teaching staff, the training needs of other staff ought also to be addressed by the school.)

The first prerequisite of this seems to me to be trust. Even when staff have been trained, there is not much evidence to suggest that they are trusted either to help identify their training needs or to learn from the courses they have been sent on. They must be personally involved in the process of identifying their training needs and seeking high-quality answers to these needs.

Meeting needs

Training to meet the needs of the students – who are the principal concerns of the school – is for teachers who are both confident and competent to do their job. It is necessary to look at separate dimensions of the consequent needs of teachers themselves, before attempting to find a way to address them. Altogether there are five 'dimensions' generally identified, as follows:

1. the individual;
2. the school;
3. the subject;
4. management training;
5. whole-school considerations.

The first two dimensions are those of the individual and the school. If new courses are being introduced (eg GCSE, A/S levels, GNVQ) or new approaches to teaching are being recommended (eg literacy and numeracy hours), then staff will need very specific training for this. If there is a general lack of management skills among senior or middle managers, then this will have to be remedied. If Records of Achievement are to be introduced, tutors and others will have to learn the skills needed to counsel the students. These needs are clear and paramount.

However, the individual teacher has needs that may not always coincide with those of the school. S/he may be at a stage of considering promotion, with the need to attend a general course for such future professional development. At one level it is possible to view such training as a waste of the school's resources, since the effective completion of this course could well lead to the teacher leaving the school for promotion elsewhere. This is a short-sighted view that is taken by schools with general myopia.

If everyone were to take this view, then individual staff will never be developed, with the consequent impoverishment of the teaching force as a whole. And if that general argument against the short-term view does not hold sway, another to supplement it is that successful schools seem to generate a healthy turnover of trained staff, who leave with their blessing: once a school gets a good reputation for staff development, and yet in turn find a much enhanced body of applicants for vacant posts. Marks & Spencer is a prime example outside the field of education of the value of acquiring such a reputation – and it seems to enhance their profitability as well! It is nevertheless necessary to balance the needs of the school and the needs of the individual.

There are also other dimensions, related to the nature of the job. Much early INSET concentrated on updating subject-specific skills, and such training is clearly necessary. However, one also has to consider general management training which is now recognized as being necessary for teachers, and there is also the whole-school or cross-curricular aspect to be considered. We need teachers who are highly trained in their subject areas but who also have a breadth of knowledge and skill that is cross-curricular; otherwise students will receive a very fragmented curriculum.

The task of the deputy head in charge of staff development is to manage a system that takes account of these dimensions in a way that produces the well trained and motivated staff needed in schools in the late 1990s and into the new millennium.

Entitlement and expectation

There is a growing awareness that staff should be entitled to training, not only to do their present job but also as preparation for future development. A clear policy on staff entitlement should be drawn up both in general terms (setting out a teacher's development needs over a period of years) and in specific terms (allowing a certain amount of funding per person per year). This is an activity into which the staff themselves should have a significant input.

Generally speaking, managers in industry not only have such an entitlement but also an expectation that they will take part in training. The damage done to education over many years by the lack of practical implementation of entitlement is that there are many teachers who do not feel that they should take part in staff development activities if they do not want to. In the long term this is obviously not acceptable but in the short term, given the shortage of money and quality provision, you may have to be less than dogmatic on the issue. It is probably a big enough job for the time being in seeing to the provision of development activities for those who are willing. However, there will be times when it is clearly essential that a particular member of staff attends (for example) a course on National Curriculum training. In this instance, the point needs to be made that it is part of the expectation of teaching a particular subject that this be done.

The problem of lack of involvement of staff does not seem to be universal. And where schools consciously involve their staff in identifying and planning their staff development, they appear to get a high level of commitment to this essential activity.

AN INSET COMMITTEE

Just as a structure for staff involvement in the distribution of finance is important, so also is a structure for their involvement in INSET management. It may be convenient to use the same 'constituencies' as are used for electing representatives to the finance committee, with different staff being chosen. Not only will this spread the burden of meetings – except for senior management! – but it will also double the opportunities for staff to be involved in important decision making.

Having established an INSET committee, it is important that it has a clearly defined brief if membership is seen to be worthwhile. I would suggest that the following items fall within such a committee's brief, without implying that committee members themselves have to carry out the detailed implementation of all these functions:

❑ preparing and updating the general induction programme for staff, including provision of staff handbook(s);
❑ establishing criteria for use of school INSET resources;
❑ identifying training needs across the five dimensions set out above;
❑ making decisions on course attendance when the request is outside the criteria set down (eg attendance on a long course);
❑ planning the use of INSET (or school closure) days;
❑ developing in-house training;
❑ advising on the provision of suitable work and study facilities for staff within the school.

Members of the committee would be charged with consulting their constituencies and reporting back to them on decisions taken. You can choose either to plan meetings a year in advance and have them put in the school diary or to arrange them one at a time. The former is probably the more satisfactory method, particularly if the committee is to be seen to carry the same status as the finance and other committees.

Since the committee exists to represent the interests of staff, it is important that they are not overwhelmed by the inclusion of senior management. On the other hand, the complete absence of senior management – apart perhaps from the staff development deputy head – may be seen as indicating that a low priority is attached to the INSET committee's work. As with finance, it is probably best if other members of the senior management team do attend but consciously limit their involvement in much of the detailed discussion. If other staff are to grow and develop, they need to go through processes of analysis and decision making instead of always relying on a 'Mother (or Father) knows best' response to senior management suggestions.

It is important that the agendas for meetings, and reports of actions taken at them, are properly communicated to staff. This communication will be performed by the representatives and by copies of agendas and reports being automatically put on the staff room notice board.

FUNDING THE TRAINING

It is a truism that no staff development policy will work without funding. When considering the programme for the year, it is important to be aware that there is more than one source of necessary funding. The policy will be most effective if a global view is taken of the different sources of cash, time and other resources.

The current (1999–2000) terminology for what used to be known as GEST is now the Standards Fund. This is money allocated for, *inter alia*, staff training and is the school's first source of funding for staff training. Under LMS, schools are to choose to allocate more from their budget share to this area. Where schools are faced with staff redundancy because of deficit, there is likely to be strong – and understandable – resistance to this happening, but where schools end up in surplus the governors might well consider adding to the INSET budget already allocated. (The examples of success and failure in industry might well be an important factor in their aiming for the best-trained staff they can afford.)

Centrally funded courses are still sometimes run by LEAs and do not cost the school anything from its own budget. Alternatively, schools may ask the LEA to manage or provide some training – for example in the use of SIMS software or IT in general.

A source of funding for some schools at least might be the business world. In most cases there is not likely to be specific funding but there may well be provision 'in kind': this would include the use of training facilities, provision of materials, involvement of a training or personnel officer, and offers of places for staff on their training programmes. The Teacher Placement Service is a useful point of reference if you are looking for contacts in industry.

In addition to links with business, there are various bodies that will make awards to schools for particular projects. In most cases these will be for materials, but in some cases it may be possible to obtain money to pay for staff development, particularly where the linkage between resource provision and the need for staff training is made.

The final source of funding is not one with which I am personally very happy but it has to be recognized that where funding is very tight some teachers are willing to contribute part of the cost of courses themselves. There are various forms that this can take: paying course fees while the school provides teacher cover for their lessons; paying part of the fees for courses outside school hours; or not claiming travel but having course fees paid by the school. If a member of staff has already used up his or her 'notional' entitlement, or a course is too expensive for the school to afford form the current budget, allowing such an arrangement may be mutually satisfactory. In an ideal world, however, all relevant training should be provided free of charge to the recipient, and I see no harm in trying to keep hold of this ideal even if we do not always achieve it.

TYPES OF STAFF DEVELOPMENT ACTIVITY

Teachers used to go on secondments, attend long-term courses, or study at one of the institutions of higher education, usually for a diploma or degree. Apart from the occasional shorter course, this was what further teacher training meant. In many cases, the study undertaken did not relate directly (or even, sometimes, indirectly) to the teacher's job in the school. This has nowadays changed completely. There is such a plethora of activities that now count as 'staff development' – some good, some appalling – that it is difficult to recognize the situation compared with even ten years ago.

One particular issue that is currently very relevant is that of accreditation. Although, in the past, studies of a year or longer earned a diploma or degree, shorter courses of study did not. There has recently been a welcome move towards finding ways of recognizing most staff training as contributing in some way towards a modular-based qualification. Some LEAs, for example, are paying the registration fee for their teachers at an institute of higher education (usually local); certain courses undertaken there then count towards a qualification. This parallels, and in some cases is linked to, the Management Charter Initiative of the business world.

In Chapter 12 we look at the National Professional Qualification in Headship (NPQH), which is likely to be a chief concern of the deputy head for his/her own future professional development.

From your management point of view it may be helpful to look at staff development activities under three main headings:

1. off-site activities;
2. school-based activities;
3. INSET days.

Each has cost implications that will also be considered.

Off-site activities

The great advantage of an off-site activity is that the member of staff is removed from the school and can be more reflective. This is also the great disadvantage, in that it is easy in such a situation to forget the realities of school life. There is a broad range of off-site courses and activities on which staff in an average school may be engaged, including:

❑ secondment for further qualification
❑ secondment (task-specific)
❑ degree/diploma courses – evenings, day-release or distance learning
❑ residential courses – often between two and five days in length
❑ non-residential courses – one day or longer
❑ placement in industry – a day, a week or longer
❑ NPQH – equivalent of up to 20 days over three or more years

The management decisions that have to be made about these activities relate to the provision of teacher cover during the days of absence, other allied costs, and of course the value of the course to the attendee and (through that person) to the school.

If teacher cover is provided, it is likely to cost in the region of £110 per day at 1998 rates. It would be very unusual to ask staff to pay for this, although unpaid leave of absence does in one sense amount to this situation. The other costs will relate to course fees, travel and subsistence.

Decisions will depend to some extent on the school's view of the value of the course to the participant. This is where it is very important to have clear policies. How specific are the identified priorities in the school's INSET plan for the year? Do you trust staff to make their own choice? Do you give them a basic entitlement (cash) each year to make their own decisions? Do you encourage evening and other out-of-school activities by not counting them against any entitlement agreed? Does the INSET committee meet to discuss every case? Where do you draw the line between a curricular course and a hobby? (An example of the latter might be a photography course, which in some cases might be of curricular value and in others might not.) Who decides that a course is important for the school and then persuades someone to go on it? Should staff be asked to stay in school when there is high sickness absence?

The basic tension underlying the questions posed here is that between staff and school needs, as highlighted in the list of 'dimensions' given earlier in this chapter. There are no universal answers, but you need to be aware at least of some of the questions and of their implications. You should also be aware of precedent –if one member of staff is allowed to go on a canoeing course, others may wish to, and you need to be clear about why the first person was allowed to go if the others are to be denied the opportunity. This illustrates the need – as ever – for future-guessing and clear thinking.

Before dealing with the very real problem of covering for absent staff, we shall look at school-based activities.

School-based activities

If INSET represents the study or activity undertaken by teachers that leads to improved knowledge, skills or concepts on their part, then in one sense we can say that everything they do in school contributes to this. This is a serious point. Every time a head of department spends ten minutes advising a junior member of department, or an experienced Year 4 teacher advises a newly appointed Year 3 teacher on an issue, there is something occurring that should lead to more effective work on the part of the learners. I do not suggest that we should log this and count it as time spent on INSET (except, perhaps, as part of a time-management programme) but it does raise the question of how the 1265 hours are allocated in schools.

This leads to the point that a significant resource in staff development in school is 'directed time'. Most schools have responded to the need for 'time budgets' by programming meetings throughout the year. Some of this time is for consultation with parents and some is usually left for staff to use, but there is almost certainly in your school a timetable of planned meetings. These may be nominated as 'departmental', 'pastoral', 'staff', 'finance', 'INSET', or whatever.

Schools used to be run on two or three staff meetings a year (or fewer!) and we cannot dream of going back to that situation. However, we can legitimately ask whether every agenda item at every meeting is crucial or whether some meeting could not be set aside for, say, a short talk or a video film on a relevant issue, or for a department to plan future courses. A lot of this does go on, but I am suggesting here that it might need a sharper focus. In deciding on such an 'event', it might be a good idea to provide tea and coffee, even if this is not normally done for staff meetings and the like, to help towards a more relaxed atmosphere for the meeting.

During the school day itself a lot of INSET is possible. A group of staff (for example, a department or a group working on Records of Achievement) can be released without causing major disruption to the school (see also 'Teacher cover' below). A member of staff can be left free on the timetable for part of a particular day each week to work with other staff on, for example, the use of new technologies. Or the head teacher can, for instance, take an extended assembly of Junior school children to allow some staff to meet.

The school can also provide its own after-school activities, either on-site or off-site. This can involve using its own staff as providers or can draw on outside sources, paid or unpaid. It is often sensible to use local hotels or conference centres, which can help to enhance the quality of the course or activity and can encourage staff to stay and participate.

INSET days

The greatest advantage of using the five 'non-contact' days for staff development available each academic year is that you avoid the problem of having to get in supply cover. It is reasonably general that the first day before the start of the school year is largely devoted to doing what a lot of teachers used to do anyway on that day, namely preparing themselves for the return or induction of students. It is now possible to timetable a staff meeting, although it is most likely to be of an administrative nature rather than for staff development. The other four days are very useful resources for staff development, if well planned.

The INSET committee has a very important role here in carrying out the forward planning. It is not necessary, in my view, for the committee to organize the detail of the days but it should agree on the strategic planning of them, ideally to dovetail with the school development plan. One tension that can arise is between activities that staff perceive as being very useful (often departmental or pastoral groups having most of the day for their planned activities) and whole-school activities that are often put in at the behest of the head or other members of the senior management team.

You can force staff to sit through a day of activities against their will (some schools may actually do this) but the whole basis of learning is that it must engage the spirit and mind of the individual. Thus the case for particular activities has to be put forward cogently, and patience is sometimes needed if staff do not immediately see the topic suggested as being crucial. If the committee is fully involved and if the staff subscribe to the school aims (or mission statement), then there is a greater chance of a shared perception of INSET needs. There will often, in the latter circumstances, be a demand for more activities than can be fitted into the four days available. But management is more often than not about managing scarce resources, and so this should not present insurmountable obstacles! Well-managed INSET days can be a very positive force in sustaining or raising staff morale and should be treated as such.

Refreshments should be provided if possible. The needs of part-timers should be addressed (if someone works for the equivalent of 0.5 of a full timetable, the expectation is that 2.5 INSET days are attended). In secondary schools, INSET days should not be held on the same day of the week each time, or otherwise a particular year group will miss a disproportionate amount of time on certain subjects. Even so, it does have to be borne in mind that midweek INSET days can lead to attendance problems for the rest of the week. It is a matter of debate whether INSET days should be 'attached' to major holidays or not; there are arguments for and against.

You should consider inviting governors to INSET days and you should also consider whether particular activities would be appropriate for some or all of the non-teaching staff.

The costs of an INSET day will be for providers (if any), for refreshments (if allowed), and for materials used during the day. Travel expenses may arise if some or all staff go out of school. Table 8.1 summarizes the costs for each type of INSET activity dealt with above: it draws your attention only to costs that *may* be incurred, not that *must* be incurred.

EVALUATION OF TRAINING OPPORTUNITIES

The real evaluation of all in-service training lies in whether or not the school becomes more effective as a result. It is helpful to make an attempt to evaluate INSET provision formally, both at whole-school level and at

Table 8.1 *Costs of INSET provision*

	OFF-SITE	SCHOOL-BASED	INSET DAYS
Cover	Yes	Yes	No
Tuition fees	Yes	No	No
Provider fees	No	Possibly	Possibly
Materials	No	Yes	Yes
Travel	Yes	No	Possibly
Subsistence	Possibly	Possibly	Possibly

the level of individual staff, while remembering at the outset that it is the INSET that leads to effective schools and that the evaluation is only a means to an end. It should therefore be kept in perspective.

Evaluation at the whole-school level

Evaluation of the total INSET programme should be a regular function of the INSET committee. Such evaluation will probably be in broad, general terms, and not necessarily an evaluation of every single course. Such questions should be asked as the following:

- ❏ Is our INSET helping achieve the aims of the school?
- ❏ Where do we see INSET going in the future?
- ❏ Are we getting overall value for money?
- ❏ Are staff needs being adequately met?
- ❏ Are there fresh ideas that we can develop?
- ❏ What do other schools do?

It is by persistent questioning that we shall get answers and therefore be in a position to make incremental improvements. It is important that the committee is kept focussed on such issues, rather than it getting bogged down in detail. Such things as teacher cover are issues for the committee, while the exact detail of the last course the head of music went on may not be.

Evaluation at the individual level

If a course is mounted by the school, for example on an INSET day, then a simple evaluation sheet at the end of the day can be useful. Incidentally, if you allow staff to take them home to complete 'at their leisure', you have probably over-emphasized their importance and yet, paradoxically, may not get them back. You should aim for a quick, ten-minute feedback session, which can either be a discussion or staff writing their answers to a few short and relevant questions about the day's activities. (Do not forget to have pens available.) The provider and/or the committee can then consider any points that emerge from the feedback for future action.

If a member of staff has attended an INSET activity out of school, it can be a good idea to ask that person to report back. However, there is no longer much point in requiring detailed written reports on every course attended. If the head of the Science Department has been out on a course for three days, the last thing s/he needs on returning is a demand for an immediate written report: s/he wants to sort out classes and the department. In other words, if too much is made of evaluation, staff will be less willing to go on INSET activities, with the consequent loss of opportunity to build a more effective school. In the case quoted, it is probably more appropriate for a written or verbal report to the next Science Department meeting.

It is a good idea nonetheless to ask staff how useful they found the course. This takes a minute or two, shows that you (as the senior management representative) are interested, and can quickly indicate any areas of dissatisfaction. If you operate in a large school where you may not see staff frequently, then a short report form might be useful; however, you should aim to keep it brief, with a few key questions relating to the usefulness or otherwise of the course.

Finally, it should be emphasized that, whatever your decision about the form that evaluation should take, the really important thing is that you actually think about your approach and that it is planned and intentional.

ADMINISTRATION OF IN-SERVICE TRAINING

There is wide variation, both at school and LEA level, in how in-service training is (and should be) administered, and therefore only general guidelines can be given here. There seem to be as many forms as there are LEAs and, predictably, some are easier to complete than others. However, some helpful points can be made.

We can look first at how the appropriate funds are accessed by a school and the procedures that need to be adopted for that process; and then we can look at how you might want to record INSET provision for your own purposes.

Accessing funds

Much of Standards Fund money has very specific guidelines about its accountability. There are many ways in which this accountability can only be approximate, partly because local identification of needs implies some local decision making and partly because schools have proved very ingenious at devising ways of delivering in-service training that were probably not foreseen.

Normally, if the school wants to access INSET money, an application form has to be completed in advance and sent to the LEA for approval. Initially, many schools had difficulties with this approach, but as they became used to the forms (and as LEAs in some cases made the forms easier to complete) they learned what type of information was required and how to fill in the forms so that approval was likely to be given.

Approval is needed for any use of external INSET money, but there are likely to be several forms for different purposes. Some common examples are thus:

❑ Form 1: used for courses set up by LEA – since the course is already approved and has an event number, this form needs to provide very little additional information.

❑ Form 2: used for courses not set up by LEA – a longer form and needs more information about the cost of the course, content, etc, and course has to be approved by LEA.

❑ Form 3: used for INSET days – needs detailed information and usually a timed programme for the day; course has to be approved, particularly if the school wants to provide lunch, providers' fees, travel, etc.

❑ Form 4: used for proposals for other school activities, such as courses or for use of supply cover to release staff for in-school activities – requires a fair amount of detail, including dates, length of activity and so on.

Unless the forms are really badly designed, you are unlikely to have great problems understanding how they should be completed. You may find that you need to know your school's four-digit DfEE number, and also that most activities will have an event number and a 'reason' code. The first will be unique to the event, while the second tells the LEA the type of training proposed (eg management, subject-based), information about which can then be gathered and collated centrally by the LEA to keep for a time for possible audit by the government.

There are additionally forms for claiming travel, costs of materials, etc and for recording attendance at the event. Once an event number has been given, this is used in the weekly staffing returns to the LEA, which then debits the school's INSET budget for the cost of the supply teachers used. It is important that the ways of accessing and recording the uses of all sources of external 'public' training money are dealt with in detail, since it is possible for the school to lose money if the correct procedures have not been followed.

School records of in-service provision

You need to organize the accurate storing of all INSET application forms and approval of event proposals. (You will then have them when somebody asks you for a record of all LEA events that staff have attended in the past year: you are likely to be asked afterwards, not warned in advance.) This record is the official one.

You may then want to make school records showing which staff have been on which courses, how much the courses cost, and so on. Keep this in perspective though; the purpose of INSET is to improve the quality of teachers, not to provide yet more statistics for people who have lost their sense of what it is about. However, if you decide you want to keep a particular type of record, the thing to do is to plan it in advance and then to devise the simplest way of recording it as you go along: this is easier and takes much less time than having to search for information after the event.

A STAFF INDUCTION PROGRAMME

The school needs to devise its own induction programme, not only for NQTs (newly-qualified teachers, formerly called 'probationary' teachers) but for all staff who come to the school.

The production of a school handbook is a very necessary activity, and one that will make the immediate induction process easier. Some schools have two handbooks, one for general procedures and information (rewards and punishments, policy documents and the like) and the other for information that changes fairly regularly (for example, the current timetable and duty lists). A simple presentation folder, with clear pockets, can be quite useful for these handbooks, since they can then be easily and quickly updated. A tip here is that if you are responsible for updating such handbooks, it is best to collect them in at the end of each academic year and have them reissued in September with the new sheets already inserted. This is a perfectly good example of the use of office staff's time.

A programme of induction should involve the relevant departmental or pastoral heads, curriculum leaders, and other staff as appropriate. It can be useful to get new staff together from time to time for general discussion, although these days there are often only one or two new staff at any one time. The key element of any staff development programme is that the clients identify their needs, and induction is no exception to this.

You should also try to build in opportunities for newcomers to see other parts of the school at work, so that all staff have at least some idea of what the total curriculum looks like to the students. It is not only subject content that can be contrasted but also teaching styles from one department to another. This can be a valuable learning process, both for the department visited and for the visitors alike. In a primary school it is important that all teachers know how children are taught in both earlier and later years.

Student teachers also need an induction programme. They can be a very valuable resource to the school, and of course the school bears a great responsibility when introducing student teachers to the profession. Do not feel that you have to do everything for the student teachers yourself: you are likely to have heads of department who know more about teaching their subject than you do (unless it happens to be your specialism), and so trust them and watch them develop their own management skills with the trainees – and if you get an invitation to the end-of-year buffet at the local institute of higher education, take the department heads with you or let them go instead of you. Be sure that they know what kind of problem in a trainee's development you would want to know about right away, and ask how their student teachers are getting on. To do this you need to keep a record of which students are in school and when.

A school is nowadays likely to have to agree that 'mentors' of trainees should themselves be trained in mentoring, and as a result – for the sake of uniformity – some schools are limiting their links to one particular teacher-training institution.

COVERING FOR ABSENT TEACHERS

Covering classes for absent teachers is a very vexed and very real problem. It needs to be said that most absence in most schools is caused by illness or by other non-INSET activities. The problem is that these are seen as unavoidable, whereas INSET can be curtailed or cancelled. Pressure therefore can arise to stop staff going on courses, even when supply teachers are provided, on the grounds that students are not having their own, specialist, teacher if s/he is taking part in INSET. Very often this pressure comes from staff themselves, since it is often easier for them to take their own class than to organize their teaching to allow work for a non-specialist.

A natural response to this situation is to downgrade INSET and to take the easy route of saying that staff must stay in school. I do not believe that this is right, even if it does make for a quieter life: we cannot subscribe to the view that teachers must be better trained and then prevent training opportunities the minute a problem arises. After all, who told you it was going to be easy? Some ways of trying to ease the problem are as follows:

- ❏ Create a 'pool' of supply teachers who know the school.
- ❏ Free a 'provider' on the timetable.
- ❏ Assign 'staff development' cover to some staff.
- ❏ Use time created when Years 11–13 have left.
- ❏ Plan courses for times when sickness is less likely.
- ❏ Book supply teachers in advance and then be flexible.

The 'pool' of supply teachers can be created from staff who have taken early retirement and/or from those with particular family commitments where a little bit of flexibility on your part may get their allegiance. An example would be where you ask someone to come in at the end of registration, which can make the difference between their being able to work and not, because of the need to get their own children to school.

If you want a particular teacher (for instance your IT specialist) to provide training for a large number of staff, you can plan to leave her or him free on the timetable on a certain morning each week (as suggested earlier in the section). This then obviates the need for cover for the specialist. If you have assigned 'staff development' cover time to some staff who have some spare time on their timetable, they can cover the member of staff who is being trained.

You know in advance when the external examinations will free staff. This time can therefore be planned and sometimes little if any external supply cover will be needed to allow a group of staff a morning or afternoon to undertake an INSET activity. If you meet objections, ask whether camps and other such activities, which cause equal disruption, are more important than staff training.

It is even possible to predict, although not totally accurately, when the pressure points will arise with staff illness, and you can turn INSET to your advantage here. Let us suppose, for example, that you have planned an activity for your Maths Department, which will involve using two supply teachers each day for a week during the month of January. Book your supply teachers well in advance and, if all goes well and (as expected for January) few if any staff are off sick, the INSET activity should go ahead.

On the other hand, if the latest virus is rampant and many staff *are* off sick (including a member of the maths department) with others struggling to keep going, postpone the INSET activity, use your supply teachers for sickness cover and rebook them for a week or two later. Once departments know that this is possible, in my experience they are very happy to work with such a system.

Allocating the cost of cover

Since the 'Pay and Conditions' Orders of 1987 (SI 1987 Nos 650 and 1433) came into effect, there is for the first time a legal framework within which cover operates. This Order sets out when teachers are required to cover and when supply cover should be brought in. Put simply, teachers are required to cover for absent colleagues from the fourth day of absence; the exception to this is if the absence was known for two or more days in advance.

There are three complicating matters, however, from the point of view of trying to operate the cover system in a school. These are:

1. It is not always possible to get supply cover, especially when there is a lot of illness around.
2. The employer has only to take *reasonable, practicable* steps to obtain whatever supply cover is available.
3. Some LEAs have reached separate cover agreements with the professional associations, which give staff more entitlement to non-teaching and non-cover time than the 1987 orders.

Your school cover system needs to be devised and operated within this framework.

A cover policy

The school – in consultation with staff, probably through the professional associations – needs to have its policy on cover clearly established and understood.

The first plank in such a policy should, in my view, be that students should only be sent home in exceptional circumstances. Already, unfortunately, there are some schools in some parts of the country where such 'exceptional' circumstances do exist and are persistent. However, these are still the exception, and in most parts of the country the competitive situation for schools means that sending children home can lead to a particular school reducing in numbers, leading to redundancies and even eventually to closure.

Having said this, it is my view that teachers already spend a very large proportion of their time on 'contact', certainly as compared with trainers in industry. They do need time for preparation. There are also times when teachers will struggle into school to take their own classes when they are mildly ill; having to cover for colleagues can be the final straw, and a teacher in such circumstances may well succumb the next day to whatever virus he or she is carrying. It is very important that senior management realizes this possibility and makes every effort to get supply cover when allowed.

Secondly, it should be noted that it is sometimes sensible to exceed the standard allowance if a number of staff are off at a time, even when strict interpretation of the rules would not allow it. Once the budget is delegated, the school can do this. Many staff will be willing to do without cover at times of the year when it is not strictly necessary (eg June/July) if they know that this is the practice at difficult times. The arrangements depend crucially on the morale of the staff and their relations with the senior management team.

A third part of cover policy should be that a system should be devised that is fair and seen to be so. There is no substitute for a written policy on this, linked to non-teaching time and other responsibilities. Careful records must be kept so that this fairness can be seen.

The final part of a cover agreement relates to the provision of work for classes. In my experience, a highly-motivated staff will always want to provide work unless they are particularly ill. It needs to be clearly set out within each department as to who is responsible for organizing that this work is delivered to the cover teacher, and a backup is also needed for when that person is off as well. If a school wants to keep its regular supply teachers, it needs to look after them. Most full-time teachers have not done supply work and do not realize the difficulties it can present, particularly where someone is asked to take a class without being given suitable work.

Some LEAs (but not many) operate cover insurance schemes on behalf of their schools (the latter funding the costs), but in very many cases it is up to schools to make their own arrangements. It is essential that a reasonable amount of money is allocated in the school budget for cover. The deputy head in charge of cover needs to have a system for recording how much cover has been used, so that the budget process can include appropriate provisions for the future.

Thanking staff

There are times during the year when things get particularly hectic and there is more staff absence than usual. A good head teacher will be aware of this and will take the time to thank the staff who have turned up in spite of being under pressure themselves. It is not only the head but all the senior management team who should remember to say 'Thank you' at times like this. It can make an immense difference to morale, but of course it will not happen if it is not part of the culture of the school.

The bottom line is that either you believe that staff work hard and in an ideal world should not have to cover at all, or you believe that they should expect to cover without being thanked for it. It is probably fairly clear which management approach I support!

STAFF APPRAISAL

Legal appraisal requirements vary from time to time and, at the time of writing, a new format is being devised. It is not possible in a general management handbook to go into detail.

However, whatever the form of such appraisal, there is a very important implication for staff development, in that this will begin to increase the pressure on resources. If an appraisal interview identifies a particular training need for a member of staff, then the implication of the whole process is that such training has to be provided within a reasonable period of time. This will in turn establish priorities, which may have to take precedence over the priorities identified for the school by the INSET committee.

It is not clear in general terms how great a particular need will be, but it has to be borne in mind. The possibility emphasizes the importance of involving staff in the identification of training needs as part of the school staff development policy, even in advance of the detailed operation of any legally required appraisal scheme.

POINTS TO NOTE

❑ Staff are the most important resource in the school.
❑ Regular training is essential.
❑ Training must be relevant.
❑ The identification of individual needs is crucial.
❑ An INSET committee improves staff involvement.
❑ The 'cover' system needs to be fair and properly funded.
❑ Encouragement and thanks to staff can work wonders.

SITES AND BUILDINGS

When we build, let us think that we build for ever
(John Ruskin)

The importance of the management of the school site and its buildings has
increased with LMS, and the latter is serving to accelerate this process still
further. A number of aspects of such management need to be considered
by the head teacher and deputy head(s) responsible, and these are set out
in this chapter.

HEALTH AND SAFETY

The responsibility of all staff to know about health and safety and to take
reasonable care to work in a safe way goes back as far as the Health and
Safety at Work Act 1974, and this is an important first point in establishing
your school's health and safety policy. There has sometimes been a mistaken belief that only staff teaching subjects such as science are responsible for this important aspect of the school; this is not the case under the
1974 Act and staff cannot ignore an unsafe light switch noticed in a corridor (for example) on the grounds that it is 'nothing to do with them'.

It follows from this that your school must have a health and safety policy, and that all staff – both teaching and non-teaching – need to be made
aware of the policy on taking up employment at your school. If your
school's policy has not been recently updated, now is the time for revision
and reissue to all staff; if necessary, some INSET time may be needed to do
this. Concern about safety does not come naturally to us in education, but
its importance needs to be underlined. There is little doubt that schools
are potentially more dangerous nowadays, if only because there is more
electrical equipment (and therefore more sockets) than there used to be.

Management responsibility

This book is not intended as a legal guide but a management one, and
therefore it is important that, on top of anything set out below, you make

yourself aware of any legislation and LEA policies that apply in this area. If the LEA does not provide a specific induction course on health and safety in the workplace, then you should contact it and arrange a meeting with one of its expert officers to establish good practice. The importance of risk assessments cannot be overstated, and it is important that governors and staff are all aware of their responsibilities in this matter.

As the senior manager to whom the day-to-day responsibility has been delegated, you need to ensure that the school policy is known and that there are specific duties carried out monthly, termly or annually (the frequency depending on their nature). It is easy to forget or ignore such things as fire drills, but if anything happens you will have to answer some very awkward questions.

There are dangers that can occur anywhere in a school (through our damaged light switch, for example) and areas where there are more specific dangers (such as science laboratories). The school policy should set out who is responsible for these areas, for First Aid kits and so on. You are likely to be designated as safety officer, while the school should have a qualified First Aider (plus additional backup staff).

There should be procedures for dealing with medical emergencies, although this is more likely to be kept under the direct responsibility of the head and/or the designated First Aider. All staff should nonetheless know the procedures to be followed in the event of such situations, which will normally involve an initial contact with the school's general office.

As health and safety officer you are likely to be responsible for preventive measures. Trade union legislation from 1977 provides for the appointment of safety representatives, who are to be given reasonable time during working hours to check that their place of work is safe. The governors should check the site and buildings at least annually, and probably more often. A general way of fulfilling these requirements is to arrange for the safety representatives, some members of the governing body and yourself to conduct an inspection termly, during which any defects that are potentially unsafe are recorded for action.

Such action may be the responsibility of the governors, in which case they need to act on it, or it may be something they need to refer to the LEA – although this situation may change in some detail for all schools after April 1999. Make sure that written reports are produced (by the safety representatives and governors) and that the LEA, where appropriate, is informed by the governors of what needs to be done. The governors should then deal with the matter at their regular meetings, except in a case of emergency when they may need to call a special meeting.

A sudden scare

While there are procedures to help you know how such a survey should be carried out, there is no legal definition of what is 'dangerous'. The test of reasonableness is likely to be applied to any decisions made in this respect. This is a very important point. If you get a safety representative (or other member of staff) saying that a certain room is dangerous (eg because of loose floor tiles), make sure that s/he puts it in writing. If the head teacher agrees with this, then he or she should consider closing that room for teaching until it has been rendered safe – or has been declared safe by an expert – for otherwise the head teacher may leave him/herself open to claims of negligence.

It can sometimes happen that certain staff declare that their teaching room is dangerous when it is not – for instance when some classrooms are getting new carpet in place of old tiles. If in doubt, recommend to the head teacher that the room be closed temporarily, pending the action or safety check outlined above.

Sometimes a scare can be started about the dangers – for example, from asbestos being used in ceiling tiles in schools, or from chemicals being used by contractors who are replacing a floor surface. If staff are alarmed, it is all too easy for a busy deputy head to become irritated or to misinterpret such alarm as being other than genuine. This feeling should be resisted. The proper procedure is to find out as quickly as humanly possible the facts (as opposed to the myths) of the situation. Do not forget also that the school is responsible for the safety not only of its staff but also of its students. It is important to act urgently but calmly.

Fire drills

There are very good educational reasons why staff do not like fire drills: they disrupt lessons, they give some students ideas for 'false alarms', and they can cause a lot of personal inconvenience. This is a case where physical safety must take precedence over educational or personal inconvenience.

There are three main purposes for a fire drill in school:

1. to test evacuation procedures;
2. to test whether or not the alarms are working;
3. to highlight the need for all to think about safety – particularly important in an institution such as a school where there is a major turnover of students at least once a year.

My view is that there should be a fire drill each term. The first of the academic year should be carried out early in the autumn term. Staff can be warned on the day or up to a week in advance. It is a good idea to have it just before the end of the school day, so that lessons are disrupted for the minimum amount of time (although coats, bags, etc should always be left in classrooms, since the purpose of evacuation is to clear the building in the shortest possible time).

You should decide the timing of the drill. If you try to get staff agreement on a day and date you will fail, since all staff in a secondary school will inevitably want to keep their 'A' level teaching lessons intact and staff in a primary school may have planned for their class to use the library. You should start timing the clearance from the moment the alarm is sounded until the last person leaves the building. All staff should leave, including any ancillaries, and the alarm should not be switched off until the building has been cleared.

There should be a procedure for classes to line up and be checked off from the registers, with any absentees being reported. If the latter are staff, then they need to be seen by you and possibly by the head; if they are students, they need to be seen by the appropriate pastoral staff. (Some secondary schools use their fire drills as a truancy check, which shows that every action can have some educational value if you think hard enough about it!)

The date of the drill and any comments should be recorded in the appropriate logbook. Ask staff to report any particular difficulties and any alarms not working. Then take action. One example might be that an alarm was not heard in a room with the television on; it needs to be resited. Do not assume that this should have been picked up by your predecessor, since the television may never have been on in that particular room when previous drills were carried out.

The fire drills in the other two terms of the academic year should be unannounced even to your senior management colleagues: in a real fire, it is not customary for senior management to get some divine warning! At least one of the drills should try to simulate what would happen in a real fire. One suggestion is that you engage the help of a non-teaching colleague to block off a particular staircase or corridor with chairs; in a fire, there are likely to be such 'no go' areas.

Equipment checks

All firefighting equipment should be regularly checked and the date of the check shown. In some parts of the school it will be necessary to have special equipment, and it is important that staff working in those areas know the type of extinguisher to use in particular situations. Such equipment is normally marked with instructions for use but they need to be read before a real fire, not during it. It should be part of the induction of staff to be shown such equipment, particularly when they work in science or craft areas of the school.

Plugs on electrical appliances, televisions, computers, etc. must be regularly checked by a competent person. Some schools buy the appropriate equipment and train a member of staff to operate it; groups of schools can sometimes share this. In other schools, they use an external contractor to do the checking.

Outside contractors

All visitors to the school should sign in and out, and all staff leaving early should sign out. This is an important safety measure because, if there is a real fire, someone may risk life or limb to try to save someone who is not in the building at all. Such procedures should also apply to outside contractors.

Additionally, contractors have other legal responsibilities, ranging from taking the normal care expected of staff to sealing off some areas if they are working with dangerous chemicals or the like. An example would be replacing asbestos-based ceiling tiles. It is important that all contractors comply with the safety regulations relevant to the work being carried out. They should be asked about this – and should confirm in writing that they meet all safety requirements – before they start the work they have been contracted to do.

Eyes and ears

Both teaching and non-teaching staff should be asked to be on the lookout for real or potential dangers. It is useful to have two standard forms for such dangers to be reported, possibly colour-coded. (Figures 9.1 and 9.2 provide examples which you may care to adopt/adapt for your own use.) There should be a procedure for reporting immediate dangers, such as broken light switches, without delay; other dangers should be reported at the end of the day. Report back to staff on action taken.

In the first case the completed form should be routed via yourself or the senior person on duty for immediate action: if a light switch is dangerous it only needs one student to touch the two bare wires for you to have a fatality on your hands. If the switch cannot be made immediately safe – and without proper equipment resist the temptation to check whether or not it is live – the area must be out of bounds until it can be. This may be inconvenient, but it is preferable to serious injury or worse.

REPORT OF HAZARD

This form should be used to report hazards that appear to be immediately dangerous or that involve electrical units such as light switches, sockets, thermostats. It should be passed to the safety officer or school office immediately the hazard is noticed.

Room/area	Nature of hazard	Comments/action already taken

Signed: _____ Date: _____

For use of safety officer only:

Date and time received: _____

Memo to: _____

Date and time: _____

Action taken: _____

_____

_____

Memo from safety officer to

The undernoted hazard has been reported to me and appears to need immediate action:

Room/area	Nature of hazard	Comments/action already taken

Figure 9.1 *Hazard report form*

REPORT OF DEFECT

This form should be used to report defects such as (sticking doors and windows, damaged curtains, lights not working). It should be passed to the deputy head teacher in charge of sites and buildings.

Room/area	Nature of hazard	Comments/action already taken

Signed: _____   Date: _____

_____

For use of deputy headteacher, sites and buildings:

Date received: _____

Action taken: _____

_____

_____

_____

_____

_____

_____

_____

_____

Figure 9.2 *Defect report form*

Defects that are potentially dangerous should be reported to you via the normal internal mailing system as soon as possible, so that you can take action as appropriate. In all such cases, make sure that any notification is made or confirmed in writing – this can be very inconvenient, but it is essential to stop wrongful accusations being made in the event of a tragedy.

RESPONSIBILITY FOR CARETAKING

The responsibility for sites and buildings often carries with it the line management responsibility for the caretaker. If this is the case, it is important that you establish a friendly but professional relationship with him or her. Complaints about cleaning or defects (except urgent emergencies such as those mentioned above) should be made through you and not direct to the caretaker or cleaner. Some deputies find it useful, at least initially, to have regular weekly meetings with the caretaker to discuss matters of note, and this helps to establish the positive and professional relationship described above. In many cases, a member of the office staff is nominated to deal with, for example, cleaning contractors.

Written reports on defects, etc, given to you by other staff, should be passed on to the caretaker and discussed. During these discussions you can also receive comments and/or complaints from the caretaker, which you also have to deal with in a professional manner for it is not helpful to the school if there are tensions between different categories of staff.

THE MAINTENANCE BUDGET

Along with responsibility for the caretaker you may be given charge of the maintenance budget. In this case you need first of all to be aware of – and to observe – the school's accounting procedures for how money should be spent. The school is not your own private firm and therefore you do not have the freedom to pay out sums for services rendered without carrying out the procedures required for audit purposes. This means that you cannot give the caretaker £20 for doing a bit of work on Saturday morning; it has got to be accounted for properly through his/her pay packet by a claim for overtime, with any necessary tax/NI deductions thereby being dealt with.

The management of the maintenance budget is a much newer phenomenon in schools than the management of the general allowance, and there are therefore fewer precedents. When an LEA was responsible for schools' internal maintenance, it was likely to deal with it in a different way from that which the school will need to do. For example, an LEA could repaint two secondary schools every year and over a period of a decade all of them might end up repainted (in theory at least).

In the case of the individual school, it will be necessary to save money over a period of time to carry out this type of maintenance unless the school adopts the 'Forth Bridge' approach and paints a certain number of classrooms every year. The latter is unlikely to prove popular. Apart from the fact that the school will always look like a patchwork quilt, it will permanently exude a smell of paint. Replacement of floor coverings, rewiring of rooms, and so on, can be done on an annual basis, as can the replacement of furniture. Incidentally, try to ensure that all departments or parts of the school (eg infants' classrooms) get equitable treatment, certainly over a period of years. You may find it helpful on occasion to take your proposals to the finance committee, which brings an element of accountability into the process.

There is some maintenance, such as the replacement of broken windows, which is in a different category and needs to be done on the basis of need. Therefore it is sensible to keep a reasonable reserve, provided that you can gain agreement that it will be carried forward to the next financial year.

Prevention is better than cure, and when staff realize that savings on vandalism will be turned into spending on furniture they may be that bit more alert at watching for small acts of vandalism and reporting them. Schools that are not covered in graffiti usually stay like that because every small example of it is removed immediately.

If your school is prone to vandalism outside school hours, you could consider employing the caretaker on an overtime basis to do small repair jobs. This has the effect of keeping the premises occupied for a bit longer and may well save money overall. It can also help increase his/her pay. You need to be aware that a lot of overtime in one week may cost a lot if the caretaker is off sick shortly afterwards. This can happen if an agreement exists that sick pay is based on the average pay, including overtime, earned in a preceding number of weeks (eg eight).

RESPONSIBILITY FOR THE BUILDING

There are many things that can come your way under this area of responsibility, and it may be helpful to mention some of them here, as set out below.

Rooms

Most departments can identify resources that need to be spent on bringing their rooms up to the standard they want. It is important to be equitable in how money is allocated and to make sure that staff as a whole know that this is done.

The senior management team as a whole needs to know about any such allocations. In a secondary school, more than one person may share the responsibility for resource allocation (whether it be equipment, staffing or furniture) and so it is possible that one department could end up getting very preferential treatment. Where expenditure has to be phased (for instance for furniture), it might be better to direct expenditure in a particular year towards a department that has not previously done well in its bids for equipment.

It is also important to talk to colleagues, since one decision may have direct consequences for expenditure elsewhere. A good example would be the allocation of a set of classroom tape recorders to the modern languages department, which will not be much use without a rewiring programme if the rooms the recorders are to be used in have only one electrical socket each.

You should agree with your colleagues about who will re-room any staff when an emergency arises that necessitates closing one or more rooms. The curriculum deputy may allocate the rooms each year, but this does not necessarily mean that s/he needs to be in charge of re-rooming. In fact, there is some logic to you taking on this role since you will be working with the caretaker in the management of any repair or building work likely to arise during the year. Agree who does the re-rooming and then make sure that staff know.

The telephone system

In some schools the telephone system is the responsibility of the deputy in charge of finance, but it does not matter too much who takes it on provided that only one person does. The siting and use of telephones can be more contentious than you might imagine, since having a telephone can be seen as a status symbol. If you are asked to take charge of the system, there are one or two things it is useful to know.

First of all, modern telephone systems can be programmed so that each handset can facilitate only certain kinds of call. Some can be used only for internal calls, some for external but local ones, some for national (or 'STD') ones, and some can deal with telephone calls to anywhere in the world. It is unwise to programme any telephone that is easily accessible to students so that it can give access to outside calls . Apart from this, decisions will have to be made with regard to the school view of who needs to be able to make other than local calls. In Chapter 7, the resolution of such an issue was referred to the finance committee, which is one way of doing it.

Whatever you do, make sure that the way in which you tackle the subject is based on a clear and understood policy. The use of telephones is a very emotive issue in schools, just as it can be in homes with teenage children. If you are not careful, it can even become a matter of principle or morality. Be warned!

The heating system

If telephones can create a lot of heat, it can be as nothing compared with the fuss created by a lack of heating. Some schools have heating systems that work perfectly – or so I am told, since I have never actually taught in one of these schools!

There is a science of heating, and in theory schools are built with systems designed to ensure a comfortable level of heat throughout a building, come rain or shine. This sounds simple, but in fact it is very difficult, for many reasons. Such reasons include the following:

❑ *Body heat*. A room that is at 16 °C at 9.00 am can very quickly become too hot when up to thirty students sit in it. On the other hand, allowing for the body heat in advance may mean the room is too cold to use until mid-morning.

❑ *Computer heat*. Computer rooms did not exist when most schools were built – and they can become very hot indeed!

❑ *Wind chill*. Until a building is built no one seems to know what effect the wind will have.

❑ *General efficiency*. Many schools have old heating systems that are no longer as effective as they once were. Unbelievably, some schools have a new heating system that is worse than the one it replaced!

❑ *Conservation*. The main problem, though, is that as the cost of heating has soared, LEAs and schools have tried to conserve energy in buildings that were not designed to be energy-saving in the first place.

Whatever the reason, the chances are that you will be called upon to deal with heating problems at some time or other. Your first need is for accurate information, and so if temperatures are low, try to ascertain exactly where these cold spots are occurring. Consult with the caretaker and the school's energy advisers (possibly the LEA) to try to ascertain what is causing the problem. Try to get action as quickly as possible and make sure that you keep union representatives informed about what you are doing. You may be able to re-room some staff and classes, but some schools cannot do this because they have little, if any, spare accommodation.

If the heating system is old, you may have an intractable problem since the cost of replacing a complete system is extremely high and it is difficult to get the necessary funding. If this is the case, it may make sense to hire portable heaters for the coldest months of the year in the same way that many shops do. In an ideal world, the building would be redesigned and/or a new effective heating system would be installed: few of us, however, work in an ideal world.

From a management point of view, you need to be calm but honest in your dealings with other staff. Do not make promises you cannot keep – and do not believe every promise made to you about the problem having been solved!

SECURITY OF THE SITE

The security of the site and buildings is important for two reasons. First, there is a lot of what some auditors quaintly call 'valuable, portable equipment' in schools (video cameras, computers and the like). Secondly, even if nothing is stolen, burglars can make the best-cared for school look like a shambles in a very short time, with all the resulting damage to morale.

Good management is based on anticipation. It is better to have a security check and a good alarm system installed before a break-in than after one. When you do have the system installed, check it. Try to walk along a corridor without setting off the system; if you can do this without setting it off, so can a burglar. Make sure that the system is checked regularly, taking care to notify the alarm company that you are doing so. It is important to know what kind of system you have. Schools used to be fitted with alarms that were activated by sounds such as breaking glass. If curtains have been fitted to the room since then, such alarms may no longer be effective. They may be similarly ineffective if the glass in the windows has been replaced by non-glass, as it may be possible for burglars to effect entry without making a sound.

Be realistic about how equipment will be stored. It is foolish to believe that staff will always remember to return every item to a central storage area every day. A large television may be safer fixed securely to a table than carried up and down two flights of stairs. An alternative is to mount smaller items securely on trolleys, which can then be wheeled in and out of a store-room.

Site rooms with a lot of equipment as high in the building as possible. Look for flat roofs, where access can bypass your sophisticated ground-floor alarm system, and take them into account in your security arrangements. Try to avoid all staff having a key to the main doors of the school, since it multiplies the chances of theft. If the head's keys are lost or stolen, have the locks on the doors changed.

Above all, ask the LEA and/or the local police to do a security check and to advise you on what needs to be improved. Make sure that staff all take some responsibility for security. Remember also that before and after school – and during the holidays – thieves are *not* at home or on holiday but out and about on their business.

Trespass

Schools can sometimes be prey to trespassers. It is sometimes amazing for how long someone can wander about a school site without being challenged. This is not only a danger to property – which at least can be replaced – but it can also put staff, particularly cleaning staff in the evenings, in personal danger. Trespassers may be people who walk their dogs (and let them use the school playing fields as toilets), or those who have a grudge against the school, or who are simply nuisances who refuse to stay away. Since the Local Government (Miscellaneous Provisions) Act 1982, the head of the school has the power to request such persons to leave the premises, and this power can be delegated. Once you have requested a person to leave the site, they commit an offence under the 1982 Act by failing to do so.

If they do not leave, you can choose to make a citizen's arrest. I would advise, however, that 'discretion is the better part of valour', and you should telephone the police. They will either ask the person(s) to move off the premises or ask if you wish to pursue the matter under section 40 of the 1982 Act. In the case of a first offence, a warning is usually better, partly because it can avoid further harassment and can also save having to go to court.

Staff need to be made aware of this legal right of schools and of the need to refrain from indulging in any remedial activity contrary to the law (such as trying to 'sort them out') – which could lead to the member of staff appearing in court instead! (There is, of course, the legal right to self-defence, but courts expect this to be genuine self-defence.)

SCHOOL TRIPS

The administration of policy on school trips is not really linked with sites and buildings but is included here as an important task that is often entrusted to a deputy head. It is important to have a clearly understood policy, which needs to be both comprehensive and written because of the potential for problems in this area.

Approval

The procedure for gaining permission to organize and conduct a school trip needs to be clear. In some schools it is customary for a trip during school hours to be subject to the approval of the head, a head of department(s) and one or more deputy heads (for example, if one deputy deals with trips and another deals with the arrangement of supply cover). The head would normally expect the deputy to at least mention to him/her trips that do not fit into the normal school pattern or that might have greater implications than usual (for example, a trip to take part in a television discussion programme). In the case of trips outside school hours, most staff are very keen to make sure that the head knows; and the head would normally wish to be consulted on any proposed residential or foreign trips.

All staff should be given explicit instructions on approval procedures, and this is most conveniently done through the staff handbook. It is good practice to have a standard form, which is returned to the deputy in charge. Figure 9.3 sets out one that you may adopt/adapt for your use if one does not already exist.

Policy issues

Very many school trips have been organized in the past without full regard to the safety of the students. All staff should know what qualifications are needed for particular types of trip (for example, those involving the students being allowed in or near water), what safeguards need to be taken, and so on. The issue of safety is one where no compromise should be tolerated, and staff should be fully aware of the nature of the responsibility they undertake when they organize a school trip.

If staff are to use their cars, they need to check the insurance cover they have; they are well advised to get any comments from the insurance company in writing. The school should have a view on whether students are to be allowed to drive themselves and/or others in their own cars: I feel

ANY SCHOOL, ANY PLACE   OUT-OF-SCHOOL TRIPS FORM

Destination/purpose* _____

Date(s) _____

Depart from school _____(place/time)

Return to school** _____(place/time)

Method of transport _____

Party leader _____

Other staff _____

Number of students _____

Year(s)/group(s) _____

Teacher/student ratio _____

Insurance checked? _____(please initial)

Head of dept. _____(please initial)

Cost per student*** _____

Voluntary contribution _____

   *Indicate if trip relates to GCSE or National Curriculum
 **If not to school, indicate alternative place of return
***If a charge can be made under 1988 Education Act

I confirm that I have taken all the necessary action.

Signed: _____ Date:_____

Notes

1. Check if a charge can be made or a voluntary contribution requested to cover the cost of the visit. Ask Jane Elliott for guidance if required.
2. Please return form to Jane Elliott, together with copy of letter sent to parents.
3. All money and invoices are to be paid through the Bursar. A collection summary sheet should be obtained and a record of all financial transactions provided as soon as the trip is completed.
4. A list of students should be published on the staff noticeboard at least 48 hours before the trip takes place; a copy of this list should be left in the office. For trips outside school hours the list should be left with the emergency contact person.
5. If the trip is during school hours and requires teacher cover, please check with the deputy head (staff) before organizing it.

Figure 9.3 *Example of out-of-school trips form*

very unhappy about such a situation and I imagine insurance companies are likely to share this feeling.

It is important that the school makes clear its policy on such issues as staff–student ratio (allowing for the nature of the trip), when a female or male member of staff needs to be present on trips, which trips need LEA approval, charging (unless the governors have a charging policy in place, you cannot charge for any trip) and the amount of notice required if a trip is to be organized.

The production of this policy must involve the head, but its operation is likely to be entrusted to a deputy head, particularly in a secondary school.

Teachers responsibilities

One issue that is often less clear than it should be in relation to school trips is that of the teachers' responsibilities for the safety and conduct of students on trips. It is essential that the person who organizes the trip takes charge of it. Other staff and students should be told exactly what the supervision arrangements are, and the standard of behaviour expected should be made clear. The value of having the type of form suggested in Figure 9.3 is that one person has to sign and thus is nominated as the person in charge.

Sometimes staff offer to pay their own way. In my view, all staff are working when on a school trip and their contribution should be paid from the charge made to students. However, there are times when more staff wish to go on the trip (say a visit to the theatre) than the staff–student ratio would require. I see no reason why some staff should not pay their own way in these circumstances, on the understanding that those not paying would take the main responsibility for discipline, dealing with illness and so on.

If the trip departs from school, then supervising staff who are not paying their own way could join it there, while the other (paying) staff could meet them at the agreed venue. However, if a teacher accompanies a trip, he cannot totally absolve himself of responsibility for supervision if he happens to pay his own way: there is still a duty of care which must be exercised.

Sometimes the children of members of staff accompany trips. If they do so, the trip leader is well advised to discuss the matter, unemotively but clearly, with the teacher and to clarify that the rules of behaviour will apply equally to all students. Just occasionally this situation can cause a little friction between colleagues. If a teacher goes on a school trip with his/her own child, the school needs to consider if this is practical and/or reasonable.

POINTS TO NOTE

❏ Health and safety is the practical responsibility of all.
❏ The school must have a health and safety policy.
❏ Regular fire drills are essential.
❏ You need a good working relationship with the caretaker.
❏ An ongoing maintenance programme is important.
❏ Expert advice on security is invaluable.
❏ School trips must work within a clear policy.

10

MEETINGS

If we do meet again, why, we shall smile!
(William Shakespeare)

Shakespeare obviously did not work in a present-day school! One of the indicators of the dramatic change that schools have undergone during the past decade is the expectation that there will be many meetings, whether of consultative groups, sub-committees, working parties, task forces, or whatever.

Unfortunately, initial teacher training understandably does not include the development of meeting skills, and very many meetings were – and are – frustrating experiences for the majority of participants. This does not have to be so, and there are certainly skills that can be learnt. (These skills, incidentally, need to be learned not just by senior management, but by all those who are likely to chair meetings in schools.) It would be quite wrong to suggest that meetings in the world of business can never be frustrating, but we can certainly learn something from their best practice.

THE PURPOSE OF MEETINGS

You need to recognize that different meetings can have different purposes. Pre-school briefings for the most part will be for communicating information, while curriculum planning meetings will be looking for debate and decisions on issues. I would suggest that any meeting can have one or more of three main purposes:

1. conveying information;
2. debating issues;
3. making decisions.

We can look at each of these in turn.

Meetings for conveying information

Pre-school briefings are probably the best example of meetings held with the specific purpose of passing on information. These vary in frequency from once a week (almost certainly on a Monday) to three or more times a week. As a middle manager you may have contributed on an irregular basis to such meetings, whereas as a deputy head you may have regular information to pass on (eg staff absence, health and safety reviews, budgeting and expenditure, and other organizational matters). And your school may well operate a system whereby the deputies 'chair' some briefings.

Such meetings will not have an agenda but should be reported in writing. There are different practices for doing this. In some cases, a clerical assistant will note what was said, which is then typed and put on the noticeboard; this serves as a reminder to those who were present and as information to those who were not. Other schools produce a staff bulletin or information sheet in advance and take questions at the meeting. (In some schools the head teacher reads the information sheet aloud, but this is not recommended as good management practice.)

At times briefing meetings can also be used to gauge feeling in a general way on some issue or other. They should also be used to thank staff for their particular efforts that week, if for example there has been a lot of illness or other cover needed. The atmosphere should be relaxed but businesslike – most people do not need to hear the staff room bore droning on every single morning about what it was allegedly like in the 'good old days'. Briefings are usually held in the staff room, with some staff seated and some standing; for this kind of relatively informal meeting this is not a problem. One additional benefit is that staff are together in the staff room, which makes a contribution to creating a common sense of belonging and purpose.

Whether non-teaching staff are invited to briefings is a matter for each school to decide. The presence of a clerical assistant to record a meeting's details ensures that the office knows what has been said. There is certainly a case for other non-teaching staff such as the caretakers and librarians being represented.

Passing on information does not only take place at briefings. Most meetings will include information, if only updating staff on what has happened to particular items since the last meeting. Three points may be worth making:

1. It may be more effective to pass on information through other means, such as the use of the noticeboards or by memo.
2. You should be wary of allowing too much of important consultative meetings to be taken up with this activity.
3. Detailed information for meetings other than briefings should be written up in advance where possible.

Meetings for debating issues

If the school is to consult its staff and to involve them in decision making, there must be an exchange of views. In most cases, however, this does not necessitate a public debate. We shall look later in the chapter at pre-planning meetings, but at this point it can be said that the activity is important, first, to establish different viewpoints and ideas and, secondly, to gauge the feeling of staff on which of these they accept.

'Brainstorming' meetings are slightly different in that they are usually seeking to generate new ideas for consideration at future meetings. If this is the intention of the meeting, this needs to be clear in advance so that there are reasonable expectations of the outcome. It is also worth bearing in mind that brains are more easily stormed early in the day than at 4.00 pm on a Monday or a Friday.

It is reasonable to allow staff to try to persuade others to accept their views, but those who really love a good debate above all else should join a debating society. The management of a complex institution like a school needs ideas that can be put into practice and that command general support. Debate should thus lead to decision making, and needs to be geared towards that end. In such an environment it can be quite healthy and even enjoyable. But such meetings should not be for the purpose of sorting out the whole of the educational world: this is for small-group discussion among staff who choose to do so.

Meetings for making decisions

Most planned meetings have to lead to decisions. As already indicated, it may be necessary to have some discussion; but when it comes to whole-school meetings, there is not likely to be very much time to uncover new ideas or to listen to everybody's individual point of view.

My personal feeling is that schools in general have improved a lot of their practices with regard to meetings, but clarity of purpose in the area of decision making is not as far advanced as it needs to be. Decisions need to be made at the right time: not too early (without adequate consideration) and not too late (with prevarication). Once staff realize that this part of the management of the school is under control, they will have greater confidence in other management areas as well.

ROLES WITHIN MEETINGS

You are likely, as a deputy head, to have to attend many more meetings than formerly. These may include meetings of:

❏   the senior management team (head teacher, deputies and possibly other senior staff);
❏   finance, curriculum, INSET and pastoral consultative committees;
❏   working groups or subcommittees set up with specific briefs;
❏   governors' working groups or subcommittees;
❏   departmental and/or year and/or house meetings.

Given this wide variety, you need to consider how your role will differ from one to the other. In Chapter 1 we looked at meetings of the senior management team; other meetings you attend will be different in that you will be present as a member (possibly the only member) of the senior management team. You will have one or more of three main parts to play, namely listening and reporting back to the senior management team, participating in debate, and seeking a decision from the meeting. We can look at these in turn.

Listening and reporting back

This is probably more difficult for senior managers than anything else! If an issue is being discussed at a departmental meeting – for example, the precise form of reports to parents – it is important to remember that this may be the only input some staff will have to the decision-making process on this point. You will have several opportunities to have your say. You need to be sensitive to this and to be prepared at times to control your urge to say a lot on the topic so that others have their chance. Having said this, if you sit silently for a whole meeting, sometimes yawning or looking out of the window, this sends unfortunate messages to staff.

You will often be tired as you arrive to attend a meeting, but so will the rest of the staff. You need to listen carefully and always use appropriate opportunities to compliment well made points, whether you agree with them or not. It is a good idea to make a written note of key points that may need to be reported back to other members of the senior management team. Try, though, to avoid it looking as though you are keeping a verbatim record of everything that has been said. You should also be on the lookout for staff who show particular aptitude or interest in a subject and, of course, you should also be seeking to identify staff development needs. Properly handled, you can also help a head of department develop her or his meeting skills – with suggestions made tactfully in the right place, at the right time, of course.

Participating in debate

Consultative meetings will from time to time involve staff exchanging views on a topic. As a deputy head, you need not only to take care in making your views clear (most easily done by thinking before you speak) but also to try to gauge the wider impact of what you may say. It has already been observed that your view carries a different kind of impact from that of a middle manager, and it is worth reiterating it here.

Seeking a decision

In an ideal world, every issue will be decided on its merits. You do not live in such a world (which might well turn out to be so boring that it would be far from ideal anyway). Therefore, it is inevitable that some issues will be resolved in a certain way for reasons other than the strength of the case for and against the particular course of action. Such reasons might include trying to give a particular member of staff some encouragement when s/he has failed to gain support in previous discussions, or trying to get from the meeting some decision, even if it is not perfect, rather than having no decision at all.

Bear in mind that you are unlikely to win the argument in every debate and that sometimes it may make sense to concede a point on a small issue so as to see what you consider as a correct decision being made on a more important issue. It helps if you try to distinguish in your own mind what you consider to be major issues of school policy (for example, the code of behaviour of staff towards students) and what are minor issues. The latter can often be details of administration that make your life slightly more difficult (for example, how a cover system is to operate) but may be worth conceding. It is essential that the senior management team sorts out the major from the minor if the school is to have a clear focus on where it is going.

PRE-PLANNING

There are two aspects to the planning of meetings in school that need to be managed. The first one is the calendar of meetings. It is now accepted almost universally that there should be an annual calendar of meetings published at the beginning of the autumn term. Apart from anything else, this allows staff to plan their other activities (including their personal and social life) so that they can attend all the meetings they need to.

There should be consultation with staff about the form of the programme of meetings and there should be an annual review so that any changes may be made. Once the calendar is published, it should be adhered to, except in an emergency – which usually involves the weather in one shape or another (fog, snow, or both).

It is not uncommon for schools to set aside a certain day each week (for example, Monday) for a cycle of meetings, such as departmental, pastoral and school advisory: it is, by the way, much easier for staff with family responsibilities if this practice is observed. Space needs to be made for finance, INSET and other meetings, and it is probably a good idea to leave a few blanks that allow for other groups to meet and to provide convenient slots for meetings that are cancelled.

The other aspect of planning meetings is the arrangements for each individual meeting. If you are chairing a meeting, sitting down at the prearranged time should be the final part of a carefully planned strategy that includes the following preparatory aspects:

❑ relevant staff should be consulted about the agenda;
❑ an agenda should be drawn up and published before the meeting – a copy on the staff noticeboard with individual copies at the meeting seems a sensible practice;
❑ papers should be produced for any issue that may need a debate and/ or a decision;
❑ the initials of staff who wish to introduce an issue should be published beside the item, and they should produce relevant briefing papers where appropriate.

Be aware before the meeting of those issues that are likely to be contentious, those that will need further consideration at a future meeting, and those that will be fairly straightforward. Talk to staff beforehand: if you continually find that meetings you chair surprise you, then you are clearly out of touch with the staff who attend the meeting. Have a clear focus about what is salient in a topic, and make sure that briefing papers have a focus also. Figure 10.1 shows an agenda for a school advisory committee meeting, comprising departmental and pastoral representatives.

If briefing papers are complex, either copies should be distributed to attendees before the meeting or you should deal initially with broad issues, with more detailed consideration being postponed until a future meeting.

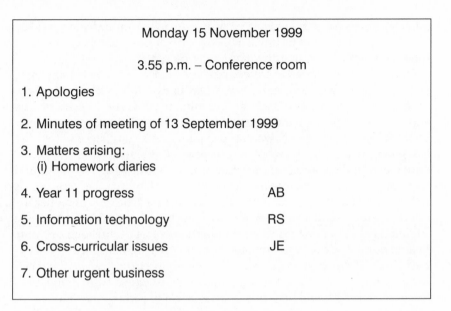

Monday 15 November 1999

3.55 p.m. – Conference room

1. Apologies

2. Minutes of meeting of 13 September 1999

3. Matters arising:
   (i) Homework diaries

4. Year 11 progress   AB

5. Information technology   RS

6. Cross-curricular issues   JE

7. Other urgent business

Figure 10.1 *Agenda for school advisory committee*

CHAIRING MEETINGS

Set a realistic starting time for any meeting you are chairing and start at that time. If the meeting is important enough to hold, it is important enough to be on time for. After welcoming staff, you should agree the finishing time (which may have already been agreed by the head teacher with the professional associations), and then it can be helpful to indicate how you see the meeting going; this would include an estimate of how long each item is likely to take. The meeting should not finish later than the time you agreed at the beginning. One way of ensuring this occurs is to have a small clock on the table in front of you, or else you can seat yourself so that you can see the room clock.

You need to set the tone for the meeting, which should be relaxed but businesslike. How the furniture is set out is very important. Most school meetings are small enough to be held round one table, whatever its shape. The advantage of this arrangement is that everybody can see everybody else, and attendees do not have to perform physical contortions to look at each speaker. It does seem easier to concentrate on what somebody is saying if you can watch them while they are saying it.

You may be responsible for some meetings all of the time (for example, the finance or INSET committee) and you may also be called on to chair other meetings from time to time. With your 'own' committee you will be able to set a pattern over time; with the others you will need to set the tone right away (even if others sometimes do not).

Once you have started the meeting your demeanour needs to be brisk and purposeful. Work on the basis that the time of staff is valuable – a one-hour meeting of 14 staff is likely to be costing the governors between £250 and £350 – and that the meeting needs to use the minimum of time compatible with a thorough analysis of each particular issue. Check if there are likely to be items under 'any other business'.

You need to encourage participation by all staff so that all views and ideas can be brought forward; equally, it is important that the same idea is not presented by a succession of speakers. There will be time to gather the weight of opinion on an issue when all angles have been explored, and you should try to summarize views from the chair before asking for a decision. Bear in mind that the best-run meetings often reach a consensus, which is more likely if the ground has been thoroughly prepared before the meeting. Summarize what you think the meeting has agreed before moving to the next topic. This will help prevent confusion or controversy later.

When you announce the close of the meeting, remember to thank all for their attendance.

REPORTING MEETINGS

It is essential that the report of a meeting is written up and distributed as quickly as possible after the meeting has been held. In some schools, reports of school advisory committees are written by the deputy heads in turn, and in others a clerical assistant does this; the advantage of the latter is that all deputies can then concentrate on the meeting and make their own contributions. Figure 10.2 gives an example of a report of a school advisory committee.

The inclusion of 'action points' in the report of a meeting can be helpful in two ways: first, it makes clear who is responsible for following up a particular point, which makes it more likely that such action will be taken. Secondly, it is helpful for individual staff, who can highlight the things they personally have to do.

The circulation list for the report of each meeting should be agreed as a matter of course, and it is my view that reports of meetings that affect all staff should be published on the staff notice board. If you chaired the meeting, you should make sure that this happens even if you have not typed the report yourself.

REPORT OF SCHOOL ADVISORY MEETING HELD ON MONDAY
15 NOVEMBER 1999

Present: JE (Chair) AB CD EF GH IJ KL MN OP RS TU VW TG
Apologies: SY

1. The minutes of the previous meeting were taken as an accurate record.

2. Arising from the minutes, there was a discussion about the use of home-work slips, which were generally felt to be unsatisfactory. It was agreed that homework is important, that homework books should be used, that pupils should be consulted on homework (stressing importance of homework but asking them for their ideas), and that tutors should not spend undue effort on chasing up homework books as opposed to homework itself.
ACTION: TU and pastoral heads

3. It was decided to do mini-reports on the Year 11 students during week commencing 22 November, prior to the parents' evening.
ACTION: EF and all staff

4. RS circulated a document on 'IT across the curriculum'. It was agreed that the English, Maths, Science, CDT, PE, languages and humanities depart-ments should nominate at least one representative each to form a working party, meetings to be held after school unless otherwise agreed.
ACTION: heads of department listed

5. JE circulated a copy of a suggested survey form to help with the cross-curricular audit, which was being carried out by the working group. After some minor amendments, the form was agreed.
ACTION: JE

6. Under other business JE reported on the decision of the governors to request additional facilities for music and drama.

The meeting ended at 4.55 pm

HJ 11/99

Figure 10.2 *Example of a report of a school advisory committee meeting*

I think that reports are usually more helpful than old-fashioned minutes. Writing minutes involves either including everything somebody said (some of which may be later regretted) or in being selective about what is included; neither is very satisfactory. In the school context, it is preferable to be seeking agreement on actions, and reports in the form suggested here seem to be the best way of carrying such action forward.

POINTS TO NOTE

❑ Staff should know the purpose(s) of each meeting.
❑ Forward planning is essential.
❑ Chairing should be done in a businesslike way.
❑ A clear focus is needed for each meeting.
❑ Decisions should be neither rushed nor avoided.
❑ Thank staff for their attendance.
❑ Reports of meetings need to be prompt and lucid.

11

TIME MANAGEMENT

To choose time is to save time
(Francis Bacon)

If all teachers are managers, then all teachers have to manage their time to best effect. This principle is no different for the classroom teacher or the deputy head teacher. However, there are differences in practice that mean that the deputy head who manages his/her time badly is likely to suffer more stress (and to cause more stress to others) than the classroom teacher. The chief reason for this is that a large part of the latter's time is managed for him/her by the timetable: s/he has little choice but to teach, for example, Year 3 all day (in a primary school) or geography to Year 10 on Monday morning, followed by humanities to Year 7, if that is what the secondary school timetable says.

As a deputy head, you will almost certainly have less teaching and will therefore have more control over how you manage your time outside the classroom. On teaching, it is sufficient to suggest that you should aim to spend no less time on lesson preparation and marking per class than you did before becoming a deputy head and that, except in an emergency, your time in the classroom should be undisturbed as a matter of school policy. It is also useful to decide in advance what an 'emergency' really is and to ensure that other staff are aware of this.

We can now look in more detail at managing your time outside the classroom.

EFFECTIVENESS

There is but one rule for managing time and that is that you should aim to use it effectively. Whether this is judged to have happened will depend on how you see your priorities. If you do not have any idea of these priorities, it is difficult to see how you can judge whether you have achieved the effective use of time you are aiming for. Being effective involves thinking first, drawing up your priorities next and only then taking action.

The following list gives a short summary of how to manage your time. I suggest you photocopy it, have it enlarged and put it on the wall in your office! Thus:

☐ Do activities such as planning when you are fresh.
☐ Set realistic deadlines for activities and stick to them.
☐ Handle information once, instead of dealing with it several times.
☐ Do small jobs when you have a spare ten minutes or when you are on senior staff duty (and therefore more likely to be disturbed).
☐ Do not procrastinate.
☐ Check your use of time regularly.
☐ Accept less than perfection unless it is absolutely vital.
☐ Finish tasks once you start them.
☐ Do one thing at a time.

Thinking

A senior manager in a school needs to act, but to act in a considered way. A danger is that because of an understandable desire to get a job done, there can be too much emphasis on the 'how' as opposed to the 'why' of any situation.

One very obvious result of this is that many deputy heads fail to delegate. They see a job that needs to be done and they do it. In the short term this may not cause too many difficulties, but in the long term such a way of acting causes others to become dependent on one person doing more and more. This eventually leads to that person becoming overburdened and resentful; in the meantime the rest of the staff are unable to carry out many management functions because they have never had practice in doing so.

Prioritizing

Rudyard Kipling's injunction, 'if you can think – and not make thoughts your aim', is worth noting. Thinking must lead to action. How to get the balance right is the challenge, and one to which we must all respond in the light of each school's circumstances. As a general rule, the more important the decision, the longer you need to spend on thinking and planning. Thus a major change to the curriculum needs more time than, for example, the way in which the students will be organized for their Rubella tests – although even the latter needs some thought if you are not to have a hysterical school on your hands!

This is why prioritizing is one of the three major elements of effective time management. There may well have been a time when every deputy head's role was so clear and the expectations of what s/he should do so carefully delineated that s/he had time to do effectively everything that came her/his way. This is patently no longer the case. Establishing priorities is unavoidable, but one reason why many fail to do this is because saying that one thing is more important implies that something else is less important. It means, in short, having sometimes to say 'No' to some of the demands on your time.

What then should be top of your list? In my book, the simple answer to this, for head teachers and deputies alike, is *staff*. It is not students! You need to get used to the idea that taking on senior management responsibilities means spending more time managing staff, with a concomitant reduction in time available for students. You do not care less about the students, but you have to accept that other staff may be closer to them and that a lot of your management of students will therefore be indirect. You should not, of course, get out of touch with the students; it is, rather, a shift in emphasis that we are talking about here.

It might be worth looking at a practical example. You may, for example, have been a head of sixth form before becoming a deputy head. If you were good at your job, the careers advice you gave to students may have been very good – better possibly than that available in your new school. You may well be tempted to take on the role that you can patently perform better than the present head of sixth form – if you see students receiving less than they should, it is only human and natural to feel responsible and to do what you yourself can to plug this gap. You may even find the head of sixth form is a willing accomplice, especially if s/he has never been too concerned about others taking over her/his rightful role.

In the short term, this may not seem to be a problem. It will provide you with a positive feeling, doing a job you are good at. However, the present head of sixth form will never get better at the job, and you will not develop properly in your own. In this context, you need to be aware of a term that economists use, namely 'opportunity cost'. This refers to the value foregone of what you could have been doing as a senior manager had you not been indulging yourself in continuing your middle management role instead. In management jargon, as a member of the senior management team you should be spending time in 'helicopter' mode, taking a detached view of the institution and how it functions. (Do not, of course, spend all your time doing this, or otherwise you will be accused of having your head permanently in the clouds!) If the head of sixth form could do the job better, then your management objective should be to enable this to happen, not to take over the job yourself.

Taking action

Once you have thought about what you should do, then you should get on and do it. Staff expect to be consulted about important policy decisions and practices, but once this has been done they will see little virtue in delaying the inevitable. The only ones who will welcome this indecisiveness are those who disagreed with the agreed action. Failing to act, when it is to be reasonably expected that you will act, quickly brings the whole process of consultation into disrepute. It also brings your ability to function as a senior manager into question.

It can be a delicate balancing act between being too hasty in acting and not being hasty enough. In the final analysis you must act on the best available information; if you do make a mistake, take the time to consider where the error lay, so that next time you will act differently. One of the best pieces of advice I received from a former head teacher of mine was, 'There is no point in making mistakes if you don't learn from them.' Management theorists are beginning to recognize that successful businesses have managers who are expected to have a 'bias for action'; making mistakes is seen as an acceptable – in fact inevitable – condition of making progress.

RECORDING HOW TIME IS SPENT

Those who are seen to be experts on time management seem to agree that one important part of managing time is first of all to recognize how you spend your time. Figure 11.1 suggests a very simple way of doing this recording, which you can adopt/adapt as you think fit.

Under the heading 'Time' you should record the time at which a particular activity of your working day began (eg 8.10 am). The heading 'Activity' indicates what you were doing (eg 'teaching', 'helping the teacher of Year 1', 'talking to head of music about curriculum'). Under the six categories, you should record the amount of time spent on the activity in minutes. Some activities will be categorized under more than one heading – you may, for example, be seeing a student and a member of staff at the same time about examination entries or a matter relating to lack of progress with reading. This will come under three headings: staff, students and admin. One effect of this approach will be that the total time recorded under the six headings may well total more than the hours in the day; it is well known that deputy heads work long hours but you will find that it is possible to work that elusive 25-hour day after all if you use this recording system!

Time	Activity	Teaching	Admin	Staff	Students	Planning	Thinking

Figure 11.1 *Time management record sheet*

There are no hard-and-fast rules about these categories. Your aim should be to establish some factual basis about how you spend your time. If the time spent on each activity seems out of proportion to its importance, you need to take remedial action. Experience suggests that imbalance is more likely to occur in the proportion of time spent on administration than in the other areas. Having facts in front of you should help minimize the risk of self-delusion about how much time you spend, for example, with staff or on planning activities.

PAPER CUPS AND ALL THAT

The Secondary Heads' Association booklet *If It Moves* (approx 1989) sets out a very salutary list of activities carried out by typical deputy heads in secondary schools (and colleges) throughout the United Kingdom. There is enough anecdotal evidence to suggest that deputies in primary schools carry out similar tasks. While I would not disagree with 88 per cent being involved in management meetings (except to wonder why the other 12 per cent were not), the fact that 47 per cent were involved in the supervision of toilets, 31 per cent in organizing refreshments and 14 per cent in ordering/distributing stationery, suggests that some schools have a funny idea of what they pay their senior managers to do. I also wonder how many teachers realize that senior management meetings can often involve nothing more mysterious or profound than a discussion of whether to have paper cups or plastic ones at parents' evenings.

Efficient administration should not be devalued; it is essential to the proper running of any school. However, there is a difference between setting up an efficient administrative system and carrying out every function of it yourself. An example is that a deputy head will often be responsible for making the weekly staffing returns to the LEA. If this information is delayed or is inaccurate, supply teachers will not be paid on time. If you are responsible for this, you must ensure that a proper system operates to carry it out. A similar thing may apply to the collation of attendance figures in the school, which need to be accurate. You need to be clear that while you carry the management responsibility, this does not mean that you have to (or indeed ought to) do the actual job yourself. It may have its attractions – you cannot be disturbed on Friday afternoon if you have to have certain figures done – but it is not what you are paid for.

This type of activity is a good example of how you need to spend time thinking out a management system that will make the collection of the figures easier and more efficient. There are management implications in any administrative system. For example, if the attendance figures are to be collated in the school office on a Friday afternoon, then the registers need to be returned promptly – and you may be called on to deal with this timing issue or to agree arrangements with staff. *This* is your proper function as a senior manager, rather than the compilation of the figures themselves from those registers.

Having sorted out in your own mind where your priorities should be, you are still faced with the task of being as efficient as possible in carrying them out. We can look at the value of a routine that may help you to manage the time you have, and then we can look at the nitty-gritty of diary planning and filing systems. Some tips on managing time have also been given earlier in this chapter.

The value of a routine

There is a difference between a routine and a rut. A routine can help with administrative tasks, while a rut disengages the mind. Routines can *become* ruts, but ideally they should be planned to achieve the most efficient operation of whatever regular activities you need to perform daily, weekly, monthly, termly or annually. I will record here the routines and aids that I use, not because it is the only (or even the best) way of doing things, but purely as an example for you to consider.

If you are going to organize yourself, you need either a personal assistant (PA) – which is the trendy way of referring to a private secretary – or a diary. If you have a really good PA who accomplishes most things on your behalf, then you ought to do the decent thing and resign, so that he (or more usually she) can get paid for doing your job. Most of us have to settle for diaries. You may find it useful to have a small pocket diary or electronic organizer in which to record any meetings that will take you out of school and any meetings in school that require your presence.

Some deputy heads carry a small spiral notebook, which is small enough to carry in a pocket (say 50 mm × 100 mm). In it you can record any details that staff mention to you about days out, students who have transgressed in some way, points they want mentioned at senior management briefings, and so on. You can then transfer these points to the appropriate place when you get back to your office, and cross them out in the notebook. The advantage of this routine is that it is unrealistic to expect that staff will only give you vital pieces of information by appointment in your office, and it is not always convenient to go to your office immediately you are told something important, but by the method suggested you manage to capture vital information imparted to you in an ad hoc manner.

The other advantage of writing it down immediately is that you do not have to remember the point made to you, only to have a routine of checking your notebook when you go into your office. This means that if another member of staff wishes to talk to you about something else, you can give the new matter your undivided attention. You may find also that staff are more likely to believe that you have listened to them if you write something down.

In addition to a pocket diary and a notebook, you may find it helpful to use a filofax type of planner in school. A week to a page, with a day page, works well for some, but you may wish to experiment with different approaches. In the diary pages you can enter all the events from the school calendar (meetings, school camp, reports, parents' evenings, INSET days and so on) and the events from your pocket diary. On the day page you can enter the things that need to be done, and they can be crossed off as they are completed.

The final thing you may decide to use if you are responsible for arranging the cover for absent colleagues is an A5-sized diary, a week to two pages, ruled. This should be reserved purely for staff absence and cover purposes, and it is always to be left on your desk so that it is accessible to other deputy colleagues if you happen to be away from school. In it you can record known absences (including event numbers and reason codes for INSET events), other activities needing cover, and supply teachers booked; it can then be used to check staffing returns each week. Telephone numbers of supply teachers can also be listed in it, although in practice one often has to telephone them at home in the evening.

PLANNING YOUR WEEK

If you have been a head of department or curriculum leader, you will have been used to planning your week around your timetable, fitting in your management and administrative roles to your non-teaching time. As a deputy head you may have a smaller teaching load but you still ought to take this into account when setting out your week. It is a myth that your new job contains so much of the unexpected that it is futile to plan.

It can be useful to sit down with a blank timetable (of whatever shape) and fill in your definite teaching commitments. Then add in your senior staff duty lessons if this system operates in your school. If you have nominated lessons for cover, enter these next; if such a system does not operate in the school, negotiate with the person in charge of cover (this might even be yourself!) on certain times when you can be almost guaranteed a non-teaching lesson. Try to negotiate these so that you will have at least one or two complete mornings or afternoons free.

You should now be left with some non-teaching time that you can fill with management and/or administrative work. These should be the times when you aim to carry out high-level operations (the thinking and planning bits of your job). Lower-level jobs can be done during your senior staff duty lessons or in the occasional time sandwiched between teaching lessons.

This general pattern gives you a framework for action. The next thing you need to do is to look in the school calendar for activities, such as parents' evenings or writing the school timetable, for which you are responsible. Working back from due dates, create your own timetable for planning and administration associated with these (allowing some slippage – see next paragraph). By filling in your timetable in this way, you may become aware that there are a few weeks when you have several things to plan and other weeks when you have less to do. If possible, you should move some of the activities back a few weeks to spread the balance over the year.

Always build in some time for the unexpected – like illness, for example. You also need to decide how much work you are prepared to do at home and when you are prepared to do it. Some deputy heads prefer to stay at school until 5.30 or 6.00 pm and then finish for the day; others prefer to break as soon as meetings etc are over and then perhaps do an hour or two in the evening at home. Some work at weekends, while others leave weekends completely free. The important thing is to decide what works best for you. If you plan effectively, this should cut down the unexpected, which if nothing else will help lessen the stress that the job can create.

An important part of planning is to remember that, no matter how efficient you are, there will always be the unexpected. Nevertheless, planning things well in advance should mean that you are able to take such emergencies in your stride, which is particularly important since it is at such times above all when a cool, calm head (or deputy head) is called for.

HAVING A GOOD FILING SYSTEM

Whatever jobs you take on as a deputy, you will need some kind of filing system – one that works well. If the school is particularly well organized, you may find that there is a central system that records all letters sent out in a way whereby they can be easily retrieved. If this is the case, you will not need to keep copies of letters to parents and others unless you have a particular reason for doing so (for example, if a parent has been asked to come and see you or if you have a continuing negotiation with the LEA over a budget query).

Hanging files

At least one filing cabinet with hanging files is probably essential. It is worth taking some time to consider the headings you are going to use for filing purposes. While doing this, remember to leave some blank spaces for the unexpected; also remember that individual files in a filing cabinet have a habit of growing over the years, and so leave room for expansion. Even with this kind of organization, you may still come to believe that any filing system is up-to-date on the day you use it and out-of-date with the next post!

Desk-top systems

How you organize your desk is important if you are to be efficient. You should have an 'out' tray, which is to be emptied at the end of every day. Nothing should go into it that is not about to go out, otherwise it is not an 'out' tray. You need to have one or more 'pending' trays, which you should organize in the way that suits you best, such as by date when actions need to be taken, by topic, or whatever. Remember the value of the waste paper bin for filing purposes: it is the most efficient way of dealing with a lot of the unsolicited mail (and some of the solicited stuff as well) that crosses your desk.

Items that you need regularly, such as a stapler and pens, should be readily accessible. There are eight items which are invaluable to a deputy head: a pencil, an eraser, highlighter pens in different colours (yellow is best if you are likely to want to photocopy items), correcting fluid in a variety of colours (for use on coloured paper), self-stick notelets, a stapler, a calculator and a clock.

EFFICIENT COMMUNICATION

When you become a deputy head, you will experience an increase in the number of telephone calls and letters you receive. Communication by these means, as well as fax and e-mail, need to be considered in terms of how they consume your time in responding to them and how you can use them efficiently. Standard forms are also a means of communicating information in a fixed (and therefore efficient) format. We shall look at these topics in turn below.

Telephone calls

You may be called upon to speak to parents and others who have rung the school to make general comments or queries. You may also receive unsolicited calls from potential supply teachers, photocopier salesmen, and so on. (The one type of call – usually infrequent – is the return call from someone you have tried to contact about an emergency.) We all use telephones at home in our daily life, of course, but it is worth thinking about their use as management tools, which is why we have them in schools.

If you have a particularly important meeting, then you should ask that calls are not put through to you. Otherwise you should use your 'Do not disturb' system coding (or button, where one is fitted) sparingly. If you receive a call you do not want, it is relatively easy to say, 'No, thank you'. Whatever you feel about incoming calls, the school office should be given clear direction in how to deal with calls, and you should observe your part of this procedure. It can also be an interesting experience to answer the telephone at times if you happen to be in the school office; if nothing else, it can give an insight into the life of the clerical staff.

As often as you can, you should aim to use the telephone as an alternative to writing. It is cheaper, provided that you learn to use it efficiently, in that it saves your time in writing a letter, a secretary's time in typing it and the cost of the postage. Before you make a telephone call you should have a clear idea of what you want and what you are going to say. It can be helpful to jot main points down on paper before you speak to someone, so as to ensure that the call is indeed productive.

Postal communication

It is difficult to understand how some people can leave their post sitting unopened for a day, or even for several days! It could well be that the letter that you do not open is the one that is really urgent. Therefore, the best way is to open post as soon as you receive it.

It helps if there is an efficient distribution of post within the school. Some letters are easily re-routed, some need to be dealt with later, and some need to be binned straight away. Be decisive. Do not leave letters lying around for days, since they will prey on your mind, clutter up your desk and will still be there until they are dealt with. Remember that most decisions can be made immediately you read the letter. It wastes time to open letters, read them all and then decide to deal with them all later. There are exceptions to every rule, but your aim should be to handle post only once.

Messages by e-mail and fax

The use of e-mail and fax are more common than they used to be. There are opportunities for efficiency, particularly with the use of e-mail. When it becomes the norm for businesses to work with e-mail, then the days of wasting hours trying to get a message to someone by telephone who has just popped out of the office should be gone.

The use of fax can often speed up such things as emergency orders, and it is cheaper than ordinary post to send messages to colleagues in other schools by fax.

Standard forms

There will be very many forms in existence in your school, for use in different situations. There are two of them that are essential if they do not already exist: one to ask for a student to be sent to you and the other to explain why a student is late for a lesson. Figures 11.2 and 11.3 set out two for you to use in these circumstances.

STRESS MANAGEMENT

Closely linked to time management is stress management. There is much talk about managing stress, but one can become stressed even trying to find agreement on the best course to follow. (I even know of a course on stress management that started with coffee being passed around; members were later advised to control their caffeine intake!) There does seem to be agreement that positive stress in itself is not necessarily harmful (for it gets the adrenalin flowing and enhances performance) but that it does need to be controlled.

I shall touch on some of the approaches to stress management of which I have heard. However, you should take these as starting-points for further reading and/or attendance on a suitable course. I should make clear at this point that I do not claim to be an expert – it is easier for those who do not have to practise what they preach to live up to such a claim.

Please ask the undernoted to report to Deputy Head's room (B9) as soon as possible/now.

Thank you
J Elliott

Name(s): _____

_____

_____

_____

_____

Figure 11.2 *Example of Deputy Head form (student to report)*

Please excuse the undernoted for being late for your lesson. He/she/they have been with me.

Thank you
J Elliott

Name(s): _____

_____

_____

_____

_____

Figure 11.3 *Example of Deputy Head form (reason for late attendance)*

Relaxation

This approach works on the basis that stressful situations will arise and that you need to be equipped to deal with their physical manifestations. Learning how to breathe properly can help to reduce the symptoms of stress; the key here is to breathe with your stomach and not just your lungs. You can try it now: slow, deep breathing and exhalation does calm the body down. Along with this, experts suggest that you should learn how to alter your posture consciously in response to stressful situations.

In addition to learning how to relax passively, you also need to take active physical exercise (two or three times a week) and make decisions about what you eat. These are preventive measures that will complement your ability to relax your body physically through correct breathing and posture. Before you start regular exercise you should have a check-up by your doctor, who will almost certainly warn you about the dangers of smoking. In school you can deliberately walk to contact members of staff instead of always using the telephone; this will have the added benefit of allowing you to see what is going on elsewhere in the school.

Particular things to avoid before going to bed are stimulants that contain caffeine (tea, coffee, cola drinks) and large meals, which will keep you awake trying to digest them. Furthermore, you should be warned about two occupational hazards for deputy heads, these being filter-coffee machines and the temptation not to have a lunch break. The former can become a habit that pumps you too full of caffeine, while the second is foolish in the extreme (although that does not stop it happening!).

Lifestyle

A second approach to stress management is to modify your life pattern. To do this you need to recognize that you perform different roles in life and to develop different ways of behaving depending on the role you are fulfilling at a particular time. Managing your time in the ways already suggested will also help to keep you in control, which in turn will make you feel more confident in doing your job. One key element in this is to become decisive: make a decision and then do not spend a lot of time worrying about whether it was right or not – it is too late.

This approach can really be summed up by saying that you should consciously take control of as much of your life as you can. Have times when you 'switch off' from work. This is, interestingly, easier to do if you actually stop thinking that you are indispensable.

Other approaches

I have outlined two of the most common approaches to stress management. There are many others, from taking up a hobby (it may not work for you if the hobby becomes an obsession), using meditation exercises, walking (which has the additional benefit of being a form of physical exercise) and so on. Some people find writing quite therapeutic, although others might find having to meet deadlines becomes an extra source of stress. You need to find what helps *you*, since everybody is different.

The best way of avoiding unproductive stress is to do a job that you like and enjoy. As a deputy head you have a fair degree of control over your working conditions, if you choose to exercise it. Finally, do not forget that talking to others can help to keep problems in perspective. No matter how difficult the situation, somebody has been there before.

POINTS TO NOTE

- ❑ You are a manager first and foremost.
- ❑ Thinking is underrated in schools.
- ❑ You should have a 'bias' for action.
- ❑ Prioritizing means saying 'No' to some things.
- ❑ You can manage your time if you really want to.
- ❑ Control stress or it will control you.
- ❑ There is comfort in being dispensable!

12

SELF-DEVELOPMENT

Our echoes roll from soul to soul, And grow for ever and for ever
(Lord Tennyson)

On becoming a deputy head you will have immediate developmental needs, particularly in the area of management skills training. Ideally much of this would take place between your being appointed and taking up post, but this is not the way things work in practice. Therefore you are likely to be taking on particular responsibilities without the necessary training. I hope this book, along with contact with other colleagues and the further reading suggested later, will help compensate to some degree for this lack of training; however, they cannot take its place.

You also need to have an eye to what you intend to do after five years or so in your new post. It is naive to believe that merely becoming good at your present job will lead to a promotion. Advancement needs to be planned, and to a large extent you will have to take the initiative in this matter.

You are, therefore, looking at two timescales and two sets of needs, those for the present and those for the future. We shall look at each in turn and, should a career move into a head teacher position attract you, details are given later in this chapter of the National Professional Qualification for Headship (NPQH) being trialled at the time of writing.

PRESENT NEEDS

The introduction of a professional appraisal system is as relevant to deputy heads as it is to classroom teachers, and one would hope that over time the training needs of our senior managers will be identified and proper provision made for them. In the meantime it is probably still necessary to identify your own needs and to look for suitable courses.

Such needs will be in the area of knowledge updates (for instance in relation to LMS or management systems) and general skills training (chairing meetings, team building, time management and so on). You should be allowed to identify your own needs at a particular time from among the various aspects of your job, and to find a course that looks suitable. You are likely to be subject to the same rules as other staff, which may well prevent you from going on all the courses that you would like to; or you may be encouraged to go on a course but find that a suitable one does not exist.

Two of the best courses I have ever attended were not run for teachers, and in fact I was the only teacher present; they were provided for employees of two large firms that generously agreed to allow me to attend. The advantage as far as training was concerned was that I could see that the skills required for effective education management are not totally dissimilar from those required for managing other forms of enterprise.

There are many other ways in which you can get the management training you need. Many institutes of higher education are now offering modules that lead to management diplomas and degrees, and you can thus make up your own course over a period of two or three years. The Open University continues to develop its INSET provision, sometimes in close partnership with the BBC.

Reading is another way of improving your skills, and specific guidance is given in Further Reading within this book. Sharing ideas with other colleagues in other schools can also be very educational. Do not always expect, incidentally, to learn most from those who are good at their job: they can make it look easy!

FUTURE CAREER OPTIONS

You also need to look to the future. For the first two years of deputy headship (unless you are in a particular hurry) you should be concentrating on getting better at your present job. Once you have managed that, you then need to give some thought as to what you will be doing in a further three years' time, and you are likely to have four main career moves open to you: headship, a further deputy headship, a job elsewhere in the education sector, or something completely different. (If you decide to keep the headship option open, you should read the section on NPQH later in this chapter.)

Headship

The most obvious next step is to apply for a headship. Having already obtained a deputy headship, you will have some idea of how to make an application and succeed at an interview. However, there are some differences of which it is well to be aware.

Making an application

Most applications for headships necessitate completing an application form. There the similarity ends. Some LEAs provide application forms specifically designed for headship appointments, while others use a general teaching form that includes such gems as, 'Have you passed your probationary year?', 'List GCE [sic] subjects and grades', and 'List extra-curricular activities with which you would be prepared to assist'. Some even send a general job application form – suitable for all LEA appointments – which includes questions such as, 'Do you have a full, clean driving licence?' In some cases a curriculum vitae is optional, while in others it is specifically banned. Some require you to apply in your own handwriting, while others actively discourage this.

Letters of application are sought in most cases, although some require them to be limited to the space on the application form, while with others they are to be attached. Acknowledgement of applications and the outcome of an application are practices that are not always adopted by governing bodies of schools: what kind of message this sends out about the school is anybody's guess. At some point on the form you will be asked for details of relevant recent courses attended; you therefore need to make sure that you do attend such courses in advance of applying for headships.

If you are applying for a job with a grant-maintained school, then there is no set practice, even with posts in nearby schools. Some governing bodies now use professional consultants to put candidates through an assessment process before they shortlist further for interview.

Giving referees

When you apply for a deputy headship it is usual to nominate two referees, the first of whom will be your present head teacher. However, when you apply for a headship in a school that is using LEA advisers to help with the process, the LEA of the school in which you currently work may be asked for a reference. Therefore you need to be in contact with your school adviser/inspector before you start applying. Some LEAs operate a fairly structured system whereby you can ask for an assessment to be carried out before an 'authority' reference is produced; when you apply for a headship the LEA therefore has a reference ready to send back.

Having your reference taken up when you applied for a deputy headship was normally a good sign, but when applying for a headship this rule no longer applies. Shortlisting is also idiosyncratic, with some LEAs giving a preliminary interview to as many as twenty applicants while others interview as few as four. The following anonymous examples, gleaned from around the country in the last few years, give a flavour of the variety of practice:

❏ LEA1 takes up an LEA reference on every applicant; does not take up other references; interviews between eight and ten applicants initially; takes the number down to three or four for the final interviews.
❏ LEA2 does not take up any reference before shortlisting; longlists eight; takes the number down to three or four for the final interviews.
❏ LEA3 takes up all references on some candidates; shortlists four applicants.
❏ LEA4 takes up references on some candidates; gives preliminary interviews to up to twenty candidates, shortlists about eight; then further shortlists three or four.
❏ LEA5 takes up LEA references only; shortlists six candidates.

Even in headship appointments there are at least some who use the telephone to 'seek further information', a practice not unknown in the educational world.

The appointment panel

Selection patterns have become even more confused in recent years since headship appointments are now made by governors. In some schools the advice of LEA officers is taken seriously by the governors, while in others there is almost open warfare between the two groups. In some places the support of an LEA officer is essential, while in others it is seen as a 'kiss of death'.

There have already been cases of a governing body failing to agree on whom to appoint, or failing to confirm the decision of a committee set up to advise on the appointment, with the need for readvertisement of the vacancy and a further round of interviews.

Interviewing practices

Just as with shortlisting, so there is a plethora of approaches to the practice of interviewing.

One thing you will notice is that the questions for headship are likely to be more general than those for deputy headship. It is assumed that you have not got to that stage without having some detailed knowledge of the curriculum, assessment and so on. For headship it is evidence of general skills of leadership, particularly the ability to lead people and to manage change, that is being sought. Interviewing panels who are genuinely considering all candidates (as opposed to those who already know who it is they want) are looking for a clear set of values and a vision of where the school might go in the next five to ten years.

The difference in questions asked at interviews for a deputy headship and for a headship has been summed up by more than one person as being between 'hard' (ie specific) and 'soft' (ie general). The terms (regrettably for the headship candidate) do not relate to the ease with which they can be answered!

The most important question

What has been said so far relates to the practices of headship appointments. However, the most important question is not asked at interviews, but is one that you must ask yourself: 'Do I really want to be a head?' There is no 'right' answer to this question because the answer has to be personal. One difficulty about answering the question is that many heads will tell you, perfectly honestly, that it is difficult to describe the job of headship until you have done it.

The other thing that is difficult to tell is whether you will be an *effective* head. This too is a crucial issue. As a classroom teacher, a head of department or a deputy head, you can be supported to do your job; as a head you are sometimes in the front line on your own, and any shortcomings you have will be apparent to everyone (including yourself). To step back from headship because you feel you are not up to the job is still not culturally accepted.

Deputy headship

The second option open to you for your future career is further deputy headship, either your present job or another deputy headship in a different school. More schools now practise team management than formerly, and in a well run school it is possible to function in a fulfilling way as a senior member of staff. There are bound to be times when the ultimate decision is not the one you would have made, but if these occasions are rare and you have respect for your head, then you should be able to live with them.

It is worth bearing in mind that some schools want deputy heads who are only going to stay for five or six years, and also that once you reach a certain age (somewhere in your forties) an application for a deputy headship is looked upon as unusual. This is not to say, however, that things will not change, encouraged by the continuing move away from autocratic leadership to team leadership. And as the nature of headship changes, becoming less school-centred and more concerned with managing the boundary with the world outside the school, so some of the functions of the head will move towards the deputies. This is already the case in such areas as resource management and staff development.

It is important that you consider your decision to be a deputy head to be a conscious one rather than a failure to get a headship. In any case, if some schools have two or even three deputies, there is a logic that suggests that fewer than half may become heads.

Other educational routes

As a third option you can follow one or more deputy headships with a different type of job that is still involved with education. Traditional routes have included becoming a schools inspector, an LEA adviser/inspector, or moving into LEA administration. In some cases secondments have been possible, which have allowed a person to try out the new job before being committed irrevocably to it and have anyway allowed a 'refreshment' break doing something a little different before returning to school. The movement to LMS has curtailed these opportunities, but there are still likely to be some available.

'Task-specific' secondments – to an assessment or literacy team – offer a variation on this theme, but these are usually for a specific amount of time. The idea of having Advanced Skills Teachers (ASTs) is that opportunities will exist for teachers to spend some time out of school, working with colleagues in other schools. If these posts expand in number, then they may prove attractive to some deputy heads.

Other routes outside education

Fourthly and lastly, there have always been teachers who have taught for some time and then taken alternative employment. Such moves have usually occurred in the earlier years of teaching, partly because the Teachers' Superannuation Scheme does not encourage leaving the profession after more than twenty years of teaching, and partly because many teachers have not felt that they had skills that could easily be transferred elsewhere. A further difficulty for deputy heads considering a move is that they may not find an alternative that offers the same level of salary or responsibility as their present job (in the short-run at least).

However, there is a trickle of senior staff who are leaving the education profession, either on grounds of voluntary redundancy or because they persuade their LEA to grant them premature retirement. The changes in 1997 in teachers' pension arrangements have had an impact on this, since it is not easy now to collect a pension before the age of 60. If you are contemplating such a move, for whatever reason, it may be worth seeking the advice of a professional career consultant; it can seem expensive but may well repay the outlay if you are really intent on leaving your present job.

If you are uncertain whether or not you wish to continue as a deputy head, then a professional career survey may help to give you some objective evidence on which to base your decision. Teaching at every level has changed since you first made your commitment to it, so it would not seem illogical to at least think about what you do as a career and whether you wish to continue with it. Some career consultants report that many teachers who use their services return to teaching with renewed clarity, vigour and commitment, having removed some of their own uncertainties about their ability to do their job.

THE NPQH

If you decide that you would like to at least have the option of headship, it is likely that you will have to obtain the National Professional Qualification for Headship (NPQH). At the time of writing it is under extended trial. At present it is not definitely required of head teachers, but it may soon be that no heads are appointed who have not gained the NPQH. Since it is in its early stages, changes may be expected, but the essential *raison d'être* of the qualification is not likely to change because there is a logical need for heads to have some formal training in what it means to be a head, before being entrusted with the job.

The existence of the NPQH has implications for you from the day you take up your deputy headship. It has been suggested above that it is not unreasonable to have a plan that might involve spending, say, five years as a deputy head before applying for headships. This gives two years to become proficient as a deputy head and a further three years to work towards the NPQH.

Who runs the NPQH?

There are two types of centre involved in the NPQH, namely Assessment Centres and Training and Development Centres, both of which are organized on a regional basis. They hold contracts from the TTA (Teacher

Training Agency), which is an agency of the government. The centres must hold a contract in order to operate, and their funding, in true LMS fashion, follows with the students.

There are two types of students, those who are funded publicly and those who pay for their own training and assessment.

Applying to take the NPQH

It is vital that you are aware of what taking the NPQH entails. The first stage is to apply to have your application to start the course supported. At present (1998), those working in LEA schools apply to the LEA, while those in other schools apply to their nearest regional Assessment Centre. This is a vital stage; if your application is not supported, you are not allowed to take the NPQH even if you wish to pay for it yourself. In the future, a failure to be approved to take the NPQH will – if the government has its way – mean that you will be ruled out of obtaining a headship.

It is absolutely essential that you get the current application pack on taking up your deputy headship. You will find that you have to provide evidence of capability in five key areas of headship, which are as follows:

1. strategic direction and development of the school;
2. teaching and learning;
3. leading and managing staff;
4. efficient and effective deployment of staff and resources;
5. accountability.

If you cannot – by the time you apply for approval to take the NPQH – demonstrate some experience in all of these areas, you may well be unable to be accepted on the NPQH programme. You also need to provide evidence of your continuing professional development since taking up your deputy headship.

You cannot, therefore, decide to spend two years becoming proficient as a deputy head and then turn your attention to the NPQH. During those first two years you need to ensure both that you undertake continuing professional development and that you gain experience in each of the five areas listed above. If you work in a school where you would not naturally have experience of, say, items 4 and 5 above, then you need to see your head teacher to ensure that you can gain the relevant experience in your current school before it is time to apply to take the NPQH.

The next stages involve having an assessment, working on files of evidence over a period of one to three years in each of the areas listed above, and then having a final assessment. There is compulsory formal training on 1 and 5 above, with optional formal training in the other three areas.

You need to be aware that the qualification can cost £2000–£3000 in fees, travel, books, etc. LEAs and Assessment Centres are allocated notional funds to help students with the costs of assessment and training. You may be supported without funding (which means you can take the NPQH but you pay for it yourself), supported with partial funding (for fees) or supported with full funding (for fees). It depends on how many have applied in your area and how much money the LEA has left, if any.

What does taking the NPQH involve?

Apart from paying out a lot of money if you are not fully funded – your school may or may not help from its budget – you have to work towards providing a portfolio of evidence to show that you have met the National Standards for Headship. There is some formal training, as mentioned, but a lot of the activities are work-related. For example, one assessment task requires a presentation to be made to a governing body. It is very useful, as with most things, to know in advance what is required, so that if you happen to be going to make a presentation to your school governing body anyway, it will be useful to know what the assessment task requires in advance, so that you have the right pieces of paper to put in your file of evidence.

POINTS TO NOTE

❑ You need proper management training.
❑ You have a right to such training.
❑ Courses are not the only form of training.
❑ The move to a headship is a big decision.
❑ There are many effective career deputy heads.
❑ You can obtain professional career counselling.
❑ The NPQH may be something you want to tackle, but careful planning is required.

EXAMPLE OF A CURRICULUM REVIEW

Schools have been bedevilled by change for the sake of change. One result has been that in some cases change that has been needed – and this book has argued for a planned, regular review of all school activities – has been neglected. Or when it has happened, staff have often been lukewarm in implementing the changes.

The key to staff acceptance is involvement. It has been argued earlier that staff do not wish to be consulted on every single detail of what should be someone else's job. However, they do have a right and wish to be consulted on major changes to their working conditions: what can be more fundamental than a major review of the curriculum, with all its implications for staffing, funding, teaching? A simple rule is that the greater the change, the greater should be the time taken for consultation and the wider should be such consultation.

In our example, we will look briefly at how one school reviewed its Key Stage 4 curriculum (the GCSE years) by involving all staff who, as an incidental benefit, gained some valuable in-service training in the initial stages of timetabling.

THE EXAMPLE

The National Curriculum was beginning to loom large on the educational scene, the school had contracted in numbers over some years and the strains on the old options system were showing. Among concerns about the future were, in particular, a wish to broaden the 'core' of subjects so that students would not make premature choices in Year 10, a desire to encourage girls to continue with physics and chemistry, and the recognition of a need to address cross-curricular issues.

It was decided that for proper consideration of the subject matter, the senior management team would need to allow a reasonable time for discussion. The process thus began with a staff training day in June 1988, with a view to implementing any changes from September 1989. Prior to this training day, all staff were given details of the National Curriculum proposals (as far as was known at the time) and eight different examples of how a 25-period week could be implemented. They were also provided with a blank sheet on which they could experiment with their own ideas.

The day started with a presentation of the reasons why any change was needed at all. This was a relatively short session (about 25 minutes) but showed clearly the inequities that were resulting from the continuation of the then current option system; in particular, it was clear that some classes were two or three times the size of other classes and that the concentration of staffing in maintaining that system was resulting in larger classes elsewhere in the school. Staff were also concerned about what, at that time, was certainly an attempt to fit 120 per cent of subjects into 100 per cent of time.

It was important that staff could feel confident and competent to carry out any change in those troubling times. Thus, the next stage was to ask departments to meet for the rest of the morning and to come up with proposals, not just for their own subject(s) but for the whole curriculum. This was an important step in trying to focus attention on the curriculum as received by the student (what I call the 'real' curriculum) as opposed to what it looks like on paper (the 'theoretical' curriculum).

The results of the morning were then summarized and distributed. It was interesting to note how much agreement there was, particularly with regard to time allocations, even though it was inevitable that there would be areas of difference. One interesting idea that emerged was that some departments suggested a change from a 25-period week.

The next stage in the consultation was to bring together the different suggestions into one single proposal document, albeit with some partial alternatives. This proposal was then put to the main school consultative body in the autumn term and the final format agreed in plenty of time for it to be put in place for the following September. There was not total unanimity, but staff did feel that there had been detailed consultation. They also accepted that change was needed – there were no calls for the status quo – and departments became fully involved in planning for implementation of the accepted proposal.

One result was that the question of 'opting' became more decentralized than it had been, with some choices (eg History or Geography or Integrated Humanities) being made at the beginning of the GCSE course, while others (such as in the areas of science and creative studies) were made on a modular basis at different stages during the course.

Footnote

An important part of the review process is that it must never be seen as having set something in tablets of stone for all time.

FURTHER READING

Practical books on educational management are more plentiful than they used to be, but much of the really useful reading on management is from outside the world of education, which you need to be able to read with both a critical and, more importantly, an adaptive eye.

The 'trade journal' is obviously the *Times Educational Supplement*: this is now available on the Internet (http://www.tes.co.uk:8484/tp/9052876/PRN/teshome.html). A very useful monthly publication is *Managing Schools Today*, available on subscription from Questions Publishing, 27 Frederick Street, Birmingham B1 3HH; telephone: 0121 212 0919. The latter is useful for the staff room as each edition deals with management issues across the school.

The Secondary Heads' Association has a range of management publications. Details can be obtained from SHA, 130 Regent Road, Leicester LE1 7PG; telephone: 0116 299 1122. Their termly journal, *Headlines*, carries useful and thought-provoking articles.

Membership of the Institute of Management brings with it a free copy of *Management Today* (monthly), which covers management issues in the business world; details from the Institute of Management, Management House, Cottingham Road, Corby, Northants NN17 1TT; telephone: 01536 204222. The publication is also available for purchase by non-members through larger newsagents.

No school should be without *The Head's Legal Guide*, published by Croner. This is the definitive, loose-leaf guide to the law as it affects schools and colleges; it is updated regularly, which is why it comes in a loose-leaf format. It is also available on disk and can be easily added to a laptop or desktop computer. The package includes a fortnightly update newsletter and an annual book on a topical issue. While it is not the kind of publication that individuals are likely to be able to afford, it is an invaluable resource for the whole senior management team. Croner publish a wide range of books and packages (including a regularly updated financial management guide and INSET training materials). Details of all these publications can be obtained from Croner Publications, Croner House, London Road, Kingston upon Thames, Surrey KT2 6SR; telephone: 0181 547 3333.

Another fairly standard publication that most schools have (although it may not be the up-to-date version!) is the *Education Authorities' Directory*. This is where you will find listed schools, LEAs and, probably most relevant for you, the addresses of examination boards and councils.

If you want a readable introduction to leadership, try *Effective Leadership*, by John Adair (Pan Books). You will find it difficult to avoid hearing about *In Search of Excellence*, the seminal book by Tom Peters and Robert Waterman, (Harper and Row, 1982) which started a revolution in the way the management of business was considered. The fact that some of the businesses cited in it as 'excellent' did not survive does not detract both from the general points made and from the continued success of the majority. The authors identify the key characteristics of success and it is surprising how many of them have found their way into management discussion as self-evident truths; these include 'management by walking about', 'a bias for action' and 'productivity through people'. It does not take too much imagination to transfer these ideas to schools.

While Waterman continues to teach and write, Tom Peters has become something of a management guru, lecturing about management to people who can afford his seminars (not deputy heads!). His book *Thriving on Chaos* (Harper and Row, 1987) does not, as you might think, refer to teaching in the post-1988 world of education but it does have some relevant points. If there is a guru on this side of the Atlantic then it has to be Charles Handy. His book on the management of schools (*Taken for Granted?* Longman, 1984) was been followed by *The Age of Unreason* (Arrow Books, 1989) and *Inside Organizations* (BBC Books, 1990). He has become even more reflective in his latest books – you might like to try *The Hungry Spirit* (Hutchinson, 1997).

A book that deals specifically with what we do as senior managers in schools is *The Reality of School Management* by D Torrington and J Weightman (Blackwell, 1989). It is more academic than the books just mentioned but is no less valuable.

While reading all these books on management and learning how important people are in the whole process, it is useful to remember that you are an essential variable in all of this. If you are feeling a bit battered at times it may be useful to read one of the many books related to assertiveness (not aggression!) A report which can be both personally and professionally useful is *Managing Occupational Stress: a Guide for Managers and Teachers in the Schools Sector*, by the Health and Safety Executive (HMSO, 1990, ISBN: O11885559X.)

More specific books, booklets and circulars will inform you about detailed aspects of your work. These change and any list is likely to be out of date as soon as it is printed. Your sources for such advice should include the following:

❑ the headteacher and/or staff library.
❑ your LEA inspectorate (where applicable).
❑ Qualifications and Curriculum Authority (QCA). (Details: QCA Publications, PB Box 235, Hayes, Middlesex UB3 1HF; telephone 0181 867 3333)
❑ The Office for Standards in Education (OFSTED) publishes various reviews arising from school inspection findings. Details can be obtained from OFSTED, Alexandra House, 33 Kingsway, London WC2B 6SE; telephone 0171 421 6800.

Educational management is a fascinating journey. If you have ideas you wish to share or suggestions for improvement to this book, I would be grateful to hear them. Contact can be made through the publishers.

INDEX